THE AUTHOR

Muriel Larson has written more than 1200 articles for about 60 different publications, as well as two hymns and one choir response.

She has had books published by Baker Book House, Warner Press, Moody Press and Pillar Books. Muriel Larson is listed in *Contemporary Authors*, *Writers Directory*, *Personalities of the South*, *Directory of International Biography* and *World Who's Who of Authors*.

Mrs. Larson has served as a home missionary for the Baptist Church, as a Bible teacher and as the founder and director of a vacation bible school. She has worked in child evangelism and participated in the Church community most of her life.

She makes her home in Greenville, S. Carolina.

YOU ARE
WHAT YOU THINK

Muriel Larson

Distributed by
Bible Voice, Inc. ● P.O. Box 7491
Van Nuys, California 91409

YOU ARE WHAT YOU THINK

A PILLAR BOOK
Published by arrangement with Bible Voice, Inc.

Pillar Books edition published November 1975

ISBN: 0-89129-024-9

Printed in the United States of America

PILLAR BOOKS is a division of Pyramid Communications, Inc.
919 Third Avenue, New York, New York 10022, U.S.A.

Contents

1
MIND OVER MATTER

But those things which proceed out of the
mouth come forth from the heart.
—*Jesus*, Matthew 15:18.

Three thousand years ago King Solomon wrote by inspiration of God, "For as he thinketh in his heart, so is he" (Prov. 23:7).

Then a thousand years later a Roman philosopher named Marcus Aurelius Antoninus wrote, "Our life is what our thoughts make it."

Thus both philosophical thought and religious record have expounded the same principle that God Himself taught when He walked the earth in human flesh. For the Lord Jesus Christ said that our behaviour and speech are governed by our hearts—our minds (Luke 6:45). And the Apostle Paul, the most outstanding and inspired expositor of Christian doctrine, taught the same truth (Rom. 8:5-8).

It is our thinking that makes us what we are. Unfortunately many people have developed harmful ways of thinking, which rob them and others of happiness and peace.

Doctors, psychiatrists, and mental institutions today have more patients than they can handle. Even professing Christians may be in such physical, mental, or emotional states that life with them and in them is a constant turmoil. I believe, however, that many of us could avoid being neurotic or psychotic or having psychosomatic ailments if we would put into effect the principles set forth in the Bible for right thinking.

Dr. J. Oswald Sanders writes:

> It is common knowledge that there are today more cases of nervous breakdown and mental depression than ever before in history—doubtless a legacy of two world wars and the continuous state of tension in which we now live. The servants of God are not promised immunity from periods of despondency if they violate natural and spiritual laws, nor have they ever been, as a study of the Scriptures will reveal. (*A Spiritual Clinic*)

The Bible says, "For God hath not given us the spirit of fear; but of power, and of love, and of a sound mind" (II Tim. 1:7). And the Biblical principles for right thinking—such as love and faith—are the exact opposites of those that are most characteristic of mental and emotional problems—such as hostility and anxiety. Furthermore, by following the Biblical principles, we can become better Christians and have a life of victory rather than defeat.

For our mental attitudes definitely govern our behaviour patterns. Psychologists who have studied human behaviour say that there are four things that cause us to behave the way we do. They are: (1) stimulus—something comes into our awareness; (2) mental aspect—we accept or reject the stimulus; (3) physiological aspect—our nervous systems react; and (4) resulting action on our part occurs.

It is in the second area—our acceptance or rejection of the stimulus—where we control the resulting action. For after our nervous systems respond to our mental inclination, we have little or no control. The resulting action takes place.

Think, for instance, of what happens when you get angry or upset about something. The blood rushes to your head, your heart starts pounding, you've got to do something! And you usually do the thing you've gotten into the habit of doing when you get angry. You yell, or curse, or say something nasty, or strike, or mutter, or sulk. Of if you're the quiet, hold-it-in type, you develop a headache or a rash.

On the other hand, if something comes into your awareness that might provoke you to anger and you have learned to obey God's Word in being slow to anger, then you have time to take the matter to the Lord and follow His leading. And He is also able to share His peace with you.

According to Webster, habit is a tendency or disposition to act in a certain way, acquired by repetition of such acts. In order to overcome a habit, a person has to develop a new way of thinking, doesn't he?

Victorious Thinking

Many who profess to know the Lord are unhappy, defeated persons. It is because their thoughts as well as many of their resulting actions are not in accordance with the principles in God's Word. Instead of obeying and trusting the Lord and loving others, they have allowed fear and hostility to rule their thoughts.

Much of this may be buried in their so-called "subconscious" and they may not even be consciously aware of these feelings. But the feelings show themselves frequently in speech, action, or ill health.

A person can take the experiences he encounters in life two ways: one way leads to bitterness, anxiety, doubt, or hostility; the other way leads to peace and contentment with great joy. If we will permit, God can use every tragedy, hardship, and problem that comes into our lives to redound to His glory and make us better Christians.

The well-known hymn writer, Fanny Crosby, could have indeed been bitter about her blindness—it had been so unnecessary! When she was six weeks old, she caught a cold which caused inflammation in her eyes. A doctor prescribed hot poultices. Fanny was blinded for life.

But Fanny's thanksgiving and contented spirit revealed itself even at the tender age of eight. She wrote the following verses:

O what a happy soul am I
Although I cannot see,

I am resolved that in the world
Contented I will be.

How many blessings I enjoy,
That other people don't,
To weep and sigh because I'm blind,
I cannot, and I won't.

Fanny lived a long life with good health and great joy. She believed that her life could not have been so helpful to others had she not been blind. She never worried, but trusted the Lord completely. And her joyous faith revealed itself frequently in the many hymns she wrote. "Pass Me Not, O Gentle Saviour," "Safe in the Arms of Jesus," "Saved by Grace," "Blessed Assurance," and others written by this victorious saint have helped many souls to come to the Lord or have greater faith in Him.

Mental Attitudes

In order to live a victorious life as Fanny Crosby did, perhaps it would be well for us to examine the mental attitudes we have which govern our decisions, words, and actions. Do we harbor angry or bitter thoughts toward others or toward God? Are we jealous or unforgiving or self-centered? Are we prideful? That's a hard question to answer, isn't it? We don't like to think of ourselves as that—but it just may be that others see it in us.

Pride is very insidious. It has a tendency to creep into the hearts of those who are especially religious. Satan, who was the beautiful, anointed cherub of God, fell because of pride. The Pharisees, who were apparently very devout men, were lost because of pride. And pride is at the root of much dissension in churches.

Pride causes us to be self-assertive, self-righteous, argumentative, uncompromising, and critical and condemnatory toward others. It leads to the downfall of the testimony of Christians.

Pride, along with other sinful attitudes, originates in the heart, according to the Lord Jesus Christ (Mark 7:21-22). The Greek word for heart here is *kardia*, which means the heart, thoughts, feelings, or mind.

In a number of places in the Bible, where the word "heart" is used in the King James version, it is translated "mind," "understanding," or "soul" in other versions. Your heart is your inmost being—your will, your intellect, your sensibilities—the real you.

The Bible speaks of man thinking in his heart (Matt. 9:4); meditating in his heart (Psa. 19:14); understanding in his heart (I Ki. 3:12); and believing in his heart (Rom. 10:9). Therefore, if the heart be not the mind, it is so intricately connected with the mind that is inseparable. (See Gen. 6:5; Jer. 23:20; Dan. 2:30; Matt. 7:21, 15:19; Luke 2:19, 2:35, 24:38; and Heb. 4:12.)

In her book, "Share My Pleasant Stones," Eugenia Price says:

> We associate feeling with our hearts and thinking with our minds. But if we pay close attention, we

soon discover that when the Holy Spirit speaks of the "heart" of man, He is including the mind and more. He means the central core of our beings ... Our mind-hearts. . . . That part of us which thinks, wills, chooses, and loves. The part of us which will one day stand before God.

Jesus said, "A good man out of the good treasure of his heart bringeth forth that which is good; and an evil man out of the evil treasure of his heart bringeth forth that which is evil; for of the abundance of the heart his mouth speaketh" (Luke 6:45).

Thus, the thought of a man's true self or heart precedes whatever he says. From his mind-heart come his actions, whether good or evil. Yes, there in the mind-heart is where the ultimate control and decisions must be made!

King David told his son, "And thou, Solomon my son, know thou the God of thy father and serve him with a perfect heart and with a willing mind. For the Lord searcheth all hearts and understandeth all the imaginations of the thoughts. If thou seek him, he will be found of thee; but if thou forsake him, he will cast thee off forever" (I Chr. 28:9).

The Bible teaches that Christians are saved by the grace of God through faith (Eph. 2:8-9) and are to walk in the Spirit (Gal. 5:16). But our wills, our hearts, determine how much we are yielded to the Spirit of God and His will. Yes, in our hearts—our inmost being—is where we first become backsliders, where we fail to have faith, where the seeds of sinful behaviour originate.

Although the Apostle Paul was the foremost exponent of living by grace, he also gave us many admonitions, rules for conduct, and warnings, which we are to obey by the power of the Holy Spirit. And if we do not obey God's Word, then we reap the consequences physically, mentally, or spiritually.

Paul continually appealed to the wills of his fellow Christians. "Put off the old man—put on the new man," he wrote to the Ephesians. "As ye have therefore received Christ Jesus the Lord, so walk ye in him," to the Colossians. "Let this mind be in you, which was also in Christ Jesus," to the Philippians. "Think on these things."

Thoughts and Actions

King David wrote, "Let the words of my mouth and the meditations of my heart be acceptable in thy sight, O Lord, my strength and my redeemer" (Psa. 19:14). The Hebrew word for "heart" also means the feelings, the will, the intellect.

Unfortunately, Kind David allowed the meditations of his heart to get out of control and go in the wrong direction when he saw Bathsheba. The lustful, covetous thoughts that he permitted to take over led him to commit the sins of adultery and murder. The time when he could have had victory over all of these sins was when the thoughts first entered his mind. And David reaped a miserable harvest from his sins.

The Lord Jesus listed those thoughts and actions

of David's along with pride, thefts, covetousness, wickedness, deceit, lasciviousness, an evil eye, blasphemy, and foolishness. "All these evil things come from within and defile a man," he said (Mark 7:23).

The Need for Regeneration

Before a person can begin to have victory over his thoughts and actions, however, he must first become "a new creature in Christ" (II Cor. 5:17). That is, he must repent of his sins, believe that Jesus Christ shed His blood for those sins on the cross, and confess the Son of God to be his Saviour.

In commenting on the Apostle Paul's call for all men to repent in Acts 17:30, Dr. C.I. Scofield wrote:

> Repentance is the translation of a Greek word (metanoia—metanoeo) meaning 'to have another mind,' 'to change the mind,' and is used in the N.T. to indicate a change of mind in respect of sin, of God, and of self.... Saving faith ... includes and implies that change of mind which is called repentance.

Thus when we come to Christ, we turn away from the old way of thinking, and consequently the old way of life. Our hearts and our mouths both are involved in this eventful transaction. The Bible says:

That if thou shalt confess with thy mouth the

Lord Jesus, and shalt believe in thine heart that God hath raised him from the dead, thou shalt be saved. For with the heart man believeth unto righteousness; and with the mouth confession is made unto salvation (Rom. 10:9-10).

Here one's mouth speaks forth the conviction of his innermost being. At the same time the Holy Spirit of the Godhead causes the person to be born into the family of God. When this transformation takes place, the person receives the potential by God's Spirit to obey the two great commandments the Lord Jesus Christ gave. He said:

And thou shalt love the Lord thy God with all thy heart, and with all thy soul, and with all thy mind, and with all thy strength. This is the first commandment. And the second is like, namely this, Thou shalt love thy neighbor as thyself. There is none other commandment greater than these (Mark 12:30-31).

According to Matthew Henry, *heart, soul,* and *mind* in this passage of scripture might "signify one and the same thing, to love him with all our powers." Or they may be distinguished as "the will, affections, and understanding."

If we loved God like that, our innermost beings would be filled with Him and His love, wouldn't they? If we truly obeyed both of these commandments, we would live in obedience to the entirety of God's revealed will as set forth in His Word. And we would be mentally, emotionally, and spiritually mature.

Victory Over Our Backgrounds

Many of a person's problems in thinking and acting may go back to his childhood. For in our childhood and youth most of our lifetime habits are formed. There is no doubt that our parents, teachers, and peers have a great deal to do with laying the groundwork for our thinking. And psychologists claim that frequently a person's mental problems do go back to experiences in childhood.

Some of the early Christians, however, came from the worst kind of backgrounds. Mary Magdalene, the woman who was privileged to be the first to see our risen Lord, is said to have been a harlot and possessed of seven devils. Matthew, Christ's disciple and Biblical writer, was a hated tax collector—one who was considered by the Jews to have sold out his people for filthy lucre.

The Samaritan woman at the well had had five husbands and was living in sin with another man at the time she met Jesus. The childhood and youth of such people can only be imagined.

The Apostle Paul wrote to the Corinthians:

> Know ye not that the unrighteous shall not inherit the kingdom of God? Be not deceived: neither fornicators, nor idolaters, nor adulterers, nor effeminate, nor abusers of themselves with mankind, nor thieves, nor covetous, nor drunkards, nor revilers, nor extortioners, shall inherit the kingdom of God. *And such were some of you;* but ye are washed, but ye are sanctified, but ye are justified in the name of the Lord Jesus, and by the Spirit of God (I Cor. 6:9-11).

Yes, the Lord Jesus Christ and the Spirit of God working in our hearts—our minds—can help us cast off the shackles of past experiences, habits, and thoughts. "And ye shall know the truth, and the truth shall make you free," Jesus said (John 8:32).

Joseph Armstrong, the man about whom the book *Light From Heaven* was written, had a terrible childhood and youth—but he grew up to be a mighty man of God. His father, a professing Christian, beat and frightened the boy unmercifully from the time he was three years old. Even at that tender age, the father made the little fellow do the work of a man.

Joseph never really knew what it was to have a childhood and to play like other boys. But because he had a godly mother and learned to look continually to the Lord, his life became a testimony for Christ to all who knew him.

And this is the kind of testimony all you who love the Lord can have, if you "let this mind be in you, which was also in Christ Jesus" (Phil. 2:5). According to this portion of Scripture, the mind of Christ was humble—even though He was God! When humility comes in, pride goes out. When Christ's Spirit *fills* our hearts, Satan and self find no room in them.

And when we apply the principles of right thinking as found in the Bible, then we acquire the peace and joy of God promised us, because we are obeying Him. In the chapters that follow in this book we will consider some of these principles, as well as other aspects concerning right and wrong thinking.

18

2
OUR WILL VERSUS GOD'S WILL

In His will is our peace.   —Dante.

Many people wonder why there is so much trouble in the world and so little peace. From whence come disease and death, wars and dissension, crime and corruption? According to God's word, it all started back in the Garden of Eden when sin entered the world. For when man chose to follow his own will rather than God's will, he unleashed a Pandora's box of evils upon his descendants.

Man has been suffering ever since. But we can't be too quick to blame Adam, for the truth is that we bring much suffering on ourselves because we also say in our hearts, "I will," rather than yield to God's will. When our thinking is self-centered rather than God-centered, we're just as foolish as Adam and Eve were.

Actually it is God's will for us to have an abundant life—a life of joy, peace, and fruitfulness. G. Christian Weiss writes in his book, *The Perfect Will of God:*

Such a life is the heritage and potential possession of all God's children. . . . Why then do so few Christians actually experience this abounding life? Why do so many grovel in the dust, never finding full satisfaction in Christ? Why do so few seem to enjoy communion with the Lord? In other words, why don't all believers know this Abundant Life in Christ so often referred to in the Bible and Christian testimony? The answer is, they are not living in or according to the will of God.

Louise K.* was attending a small church near her home. It was convenient for her. It only took five minutes to get there. The services lasted less than an hour. And Sunday School was held during church service, which she considered very advantageous as far as her active young child was concerned. The only trouble was, she wasn't happy. She felt as if she should be doing something for the Lord, and she wasn't.

She went to the Lord in prayer about the matter. And it seemed as if the Lord were saying to her, "Do you want your own convenience, or do you really desire My will for your life?" As Louise faced that question squarely, she yielded to the Lord and sought His will. Not long after that, the Lord led her to a church clear across town, where her musical and teaching ability were immediately *put to work*. Seeking and finding God's will brought Louise great peace, joy, and fruitfulness.

Now on the surface it would appear that Louise was doing no great wrong in attending a good

*Fictitious name.

church that was convenient to her. But act~
she was setting her will—her desire for
nience—against God's will for her life. A
the basic problem in every case whe~
does not have an abundant life.

The Bible says, "Delight thyself also i~
Lord; and he shall give thee the desires of thin~
heart. Commit thy way unto the Lord; trust also
in him; and he shall bring it to pass" (Psa. 37:4-
5).

There are basically two types of people whose
lives aren't yielded to the Lord and who, therefore,
do not have the peace and joy of the Lord. These
are known in Christian theology as the natural man
(I Cor. 2:14) and the carnal Christian (I Cor.
3:1). Ruth Paxson wrote:

> There are two pictures before us. One is the pic-
> ture of a Satan-controlled, a world-conformed and
> a flesh-centered life. The other is the picture of a
> Christ-controlled; Christ-conformed; Christ-cen-
> tered life.—*Called Unto Holiness.*

The person who has never taken the first step of
yielding to God—that is, by accepting Jesus Christ
as his Saviour (John 3:16-18)—is completely in
the first picture. The carnal Christian is often in
the first picture, but knows in his heart that he
ought to be in the second. Therefore deep down inside, he's miserable!

This very conflict disturbs the mind's proper bal-
ance. Thus this person's life is a stumbling block to
others. But often such a person will keep himself
very busy so that he'll have no time to think.

However, it's human nature for us to hang on to our self-life, isn't it? That part of us is always battling against the spirit. "Submission and suffering are utterly contrary to the flesh," wrote L.E. Maxwell. "The thing man loves more than anything else in the world is himself. The thing man wants is to have his own way and to enjoy himself" (*Born Crucified*).

What we need to grasp with our understanding is that our greatest good lies in yielding to God and letting Him have His way in everything in our lives. He loves us. He loved us so much that He died for us (I John 3:16). The Bible says that He works all things for good to those of us who love Him and are called according to His purpose (Rom. 8:28).

In his book *The Way of Victory* James H. McConkey told of a great engineer who lay dying—

> He had been one of the most brilliant men of his generation. His genius had wrought wonderful achievements in his chosen profession. Most men would look with envy upon what he had accomplished. But as the clergyman friend sat with him in his last hours he said soberly to that friend, "Mr. E—, now that I have come to the end of it all I realize that I have all my life been doing second things."

Yielding to God's Will

Mr. McConkey said in his book, *The Three-Fold Secret of the Holy Spirit*, that this secret consists of the incoming of the Holy Spirit when a person believes in Christ, the granting of the fullness of the Spirit when he yields to Christ; and the constant manifestation of the Spirit when he abides in Christ.

The initial coming to Christ and acknowledging that He alone can save us from our sins is in effect saying, "Here I am, Lord. I'm helpless to save myself. I'm turning away from my sinful life toward You." At this submission God the Holy Spirit enters into us. This is why we often hear such wonderful testimonies of men and women being miraculously delivered from alcoholism, drug addiction, and sin of all kinds.

Some years ago with the help of a friend I held a service for the women in the Elizabeth (N.J.) County Jail. We had the joy of leading four women to Christ, including one named Marie.

"Did that dark-haired young woman give you any trouble?" asked the matron as my friend and I were leaving. "She's the worst character we've ever had in this jail."

"No," I answered. "As a matter of fact she accepted Christ as her Saviour today." The matron shook her head in unbelief.

But the next time we came back she remarked, "I don't know what you people said to that Marie, but she sure has been a different person since the last time you were here!"

Several months later I received a letter from Marie, who had been sent to the state prison. She wrote, "I thank Jesus for giving my husband and two little girls back to me. Also I know you'll be happy to hear that I was made the honor girl of my cottage."

As long as we are in the flesh, however, we still have our old Adamic nature. This is in conflict with our new spiritual nature, and thus we have a war going on (Gal. 5:17-18). As the old Indian told the missionary, it's like two dogs fighting at times. When the missionary asked which one won, the Indian answered, "Whichever one I say 'Sic 'em.' "

The reason why so many new converts can give exciting testimonies of the victory of God over sin in their lives is because at the time of their conversation they were completely yielded to the will of God. After a while, however, many allow sin, self, or Satan to detour them. They lose their first love.

The Apostle Paul advocates the following to those who are already Christians:

> I beseech you therefore, brethren, by the mercies of God, that ye present your bodies a living sacrifice, holy, acceptable unto God, which is your reasonable service. And be not conformed to this world; but be ye transformed by the renewing of your mind, that ye may prove what is that good, and acceptable, and perfect, will of God (Rom. 12:1-2).

This definite act of committal takes place when a person dedicates or consecrates his life to Christ. In some cases it takes place even when a person is born again. Note that the verse says you are not to be conformed to the world, but are to be transformed by the renewing of your *mind*, "so as to find and follow God's will," according to the Williams New Testamant.

In her hook, *The Christian's Secret of a Happy Life*, Hannah Whitall Smith wrote:

> I am convinced that throughout the Bible the expressions concerning the "heart" do not mean the emotions, that which we now understand by the word "heart," but they mean the will, the personality of the man, the man's own central self; and that the object of God's dealings with man is that this "I" may be yielded up to Him, and this central life abandoned to His entire control. It is not the feelings of the man God wants, but the man himself.

When we are fully yielded to God, then we are filled with the Holy Spirit. Deserting the world and all of its fleshly ideas, we are transformed by the renewal of our minds. We desire to do God's will with all our hearts. When we're filled with the Spirit, we have power from God to live victorious lives and accomplish great things for His glory.

Our Lord Jesus Christ, God's son, lived the perfect life here on earth. He also gave us the perfect prayer, in which He said, "Thy will be done" (Matt. 6:10).

"In Christ and His example God has revealed the devotion to and the delight in His will which He asks and expects of us," Andrew Murray wrote. "In Christ and His Spirit He renews and takes possession of our will: works in it both to will and to do, making us able and willing to do all His will" (*Triumph in the Inner Life*).

How is it then that we who have dedicated our bodies and our lives to God fail at times to live a victorious life? How is it that we fail to do His will, lose our enthusiasm for His work and for winning souls, and fall back into old shortcomings? The answer is that we have failed to abide in Christ. As McConkey taught, the Spirit is constantly manifested when we are abiding in Him.

What hinders the Spirit from being manifested in us? We stray from the will of God, we stray from our love for Him, we stray from full committal. We disobey God. We grieve the Holy Spirit with sinful behaviour, or we quench Him when He reveals God's will for us. The fault lies in our heart-minds.

The Bible says. "Be not wise in your own eyes; reverently fear and worship the Lord, and turn [entirely] away from evil.... It shall be health to your nerves and sinews, and marrow and moistening to your bones" (Prov. 3:7-8, *The Amplified Old Testament*, Zondervan, 1962).

Abiding in Christ is daily walking with Him, daily committal to Him, daily yielding our wills to His. The abundant life He promised can only be had by abiding in Him. The Bible says, "And the world passeth away, and the lust thereof, but he that doeth the will of God abideth forever" (I John 2:17).

How to Know God's Will

Jesus said, "If any man will do his will, he shall know . . ." (John 7:17). He also promised, "Howbeit when he, the Spirit of truth, is come, he will guide you into all truth . . ." (John 16:13).

It is God's will for us to know His will, but our minds have to be open and receptive to it. Dr. Lewis Sperry Shaeffer wrote, "God always speaks loud enough to make a willing soul hear!"

But if our minds are clogged with sinful or self-centered thoughts, then our receiving station needs an overhauling. This can be accomplished by the mechanics of humility and submission and a clean sweep on our knees. The Bible says, "If we confess our sins, he is faithful and just to forgive us our sins and to cleanse us from all unrighteousness" (I John 1:9). The First step to knowing God's will, according to that great man of faith George Mueller, is to surrender our wills to God.

Mueller said, "I seek the will of the Spirit of God through, or in connection with, the Word of God. The Spirit and the Word must be combined. If I look to the Spirit alone without the Word, I lay myself open to great delusions also. If the Holy Ghost guides us at all, He will do it according to the Scriptures and never contrary to them." This man of God also took into account providential circumstances and prayed to the Lord to reveal His will.

"In trivial matters and in transactions involving most important issues I have found this method always effective," he avowed. Certainly the outstanding example of George Mueller's life of faith, the success of his orphanage work, and the many answers to prayer he received attest to the efficacy of his method!

The Apostle Paul wrote to the Colossian Christians:

... I have never ceased praying for you and asking God to fill you, through full wisdom and spiritual insight, with a clear knowledge of His will, so that you may lead lives worthy of the Lord to His full satisfaction, by perennially bearing fruit in every good enterprise and by a steady growth in a fuller knowledge of God ... (Col. 1:9-10, *Williams N.T.*).

A knowledge of God's Word helps us to lead fruitful lives worthy of the Lord and to better know his will for each step of our way. For God often speaks to our hearts through His word.

Adoniram Judson, for instance, felt certain that God was calling him to be a missionary to India, after reading a certain book. After a while, however, doubts crept in and he wondered, *If God wants me to go to India, would He stop speaking and leave me in this awful silence?*

Adoniram reached down to the muddy ground on which he was standing to pick up a fallen leaf. In that instant the Bible verse came to him, "Go ye into all the world and preach the gospel." He heard it as clearly as if someone had spoken! And he knew his calling was sure. Even though family and friends pleaded with him to take a plush pastorate offered him in Boston, he turned it down.

Later, when God led Adoniram and his bride out to the Far East, He permitted the door to be shut to India—but opened it to Burma. That was a providential circumstance. Adoniram was used of God to open all of Burma to the Gospel of Jesus Christ.

R.A. Torrey said, "The main point in the whole matter of guidance is absolute surrender of the will to God, delighting in His will, and willingness to do joyfully the very things we would not like to do naturally."

A careful way of living is God's will for every Christian. The Bible says, "See then that ye walk circumspectly, not as fools, but as wise, redeeming the time, because the days are evil. Wherefore be ye not unwise, but understanding what the will of the Lord is" (Eph. 5:15-17).

There are certain principles which God lays down in His Word that prescribe the circumspect walk for the Christian. According to James, we are to be doers of the word, not hearers only, deceiving ourselves (Jas. 1:22).

We are to walk not after the flesh but after the spirit (Rom. 8). Ephesians 4 and 5 and Colossians 3 explain in detail how to do this.

We are told not to have close relationships with people who do not love the Lord (II Cor. 6:14-18). We are admonished to be holy (I Pet. 1:16); to avoid being stumbling blocks to others (Rom. 14:13); to do all to the glory of God (I Cor.10:31); to take proper care of our bodies (I Cor. 6:19-20). And we are to love one another, truly love one another (I John 4:7).

To know God's will for much of our daily walk, therefore, we need to read His Word regularly. It is our guideline and by it the Spirit speaks to us and leads us in the way we should go. As we take its instruction into our minds, our lives are affected accordingly.

Jesus, the Son of God, said, "Blessed are they

that hear the word of God and keep it" (Luke 11:28).

> With patient mind thy course of duty run,
> God nothing does nor suffers to be done,
> But thou wouldst do thyself,
> If thou couldst see the end of all events as well as
> He. —Anon.

3
GOOD THINKING

This book of the law shall not depart out of thy mouth; but thou shalt meditate therein day and night, that thou mayest observe to do according to all that is written therein; for then thou shalt make thy way prosperous, and then thou shalt have good success. —Joshua 1:8.

Good thinking leads to a successful life. Right thinking helps you to live in harmony with your fellow men. Meditation day and night on God's Word and His requirements for a righteous life will instill in you a keen desire to overcome your shortcomings and please God in all that you do. This in turn will help you to have a life of peace and joy.

What do you meditate about day and night? Are your thoughts self-centered? Do they revolve around yourself and your plans? Are they daydreams that build up your ego? Are they ill, angry thoughts against others? Or are they conformed to the standard of God's Word? Part of that standard is found in Philippians 4:8-9—

31

> Finally, brethren, whatsoever things are true, whatsoever things are honest, whatsoever things are just, whatsoever things are pure, whatsoever things are lovely, whatsoever things are of good report; if there be any virtue, and if there be any praise, think on these things. Those things which ye have both learned and received and heard and seen in me, do: and the God of peace shall be with you.

The promise for following this wise, Godgiven piece of advice is that you will enjoy the presence and peace of God.

Mary Slessor, the courageous, red-haired missionary who became known as the "White Queen of the Cannibals," wrote home to friends in Scotland about the victorious life of a native woman in Africa:

> She is so poor that she has not one farthing in this world but what she gets from us, not a creature to do a thing for her, her house all open to rain and ruin, and into which the cows rush at times. But blind Mary is our living, bright, clear light.... The other day I heard the chief say that she was the only visible witness among the church members in the town, but he added, 'She is a proper one.' Far advanced in spiritual knowledge and experience she knows the deep things of God. That old hut is like a heaven here to more than me.

Just think of being blind and desperately poor, of having cows stomp through your house before you realize what is happening, of having rain and dirt sweep in at will! If anyone had reason to be bitter or complain or think ill thoughts, this woman did. But Mary also wrote about her—

> Her voice is set to music, a miracle to the people here who know only how to groan and grumble. She is ever praising the Lord and her testimony to the Saviour is not a shabby one.

We must be convinced that this admirable African woman meditated on God and His Word day and night. It was her very life. And so that dedicated servant of God, Mary Slessor, found joy and refreshment in that blind woman's tumbled-down hut—"like a heaven here to more than me," she wrote.

Say, is your home like heaven to the other members of your family, as well as to those who visit, because of your sweet, rejoicing life? There is no reason it shouldn't be, is there?

We think laughingly of "the good old days" when men had to harness and unharness horses and women had to do their washing on an old scrub-board. But my mother tells me of how her mother, who was beset by troubles, used to comfort herself by singing gospel hymns as she bent over her scrub-board. She was trying to keep her mind off her troubles and on the precious promises of God. Not many of us go around singing the old hymns these days, do we? Perhaps if we did, they would lift our minds to higher planes!

True and Honest Thinking

Think on things that are true, the Bible verse says. What is true? God is true, His word is true, His salvation and promises are true. Nothing better could we think about or meditate on than these.

The Bible calls our God "a God of truth" (Deut. 32:4). Jesus Christ, the Son of God, said, "I am the way, the truth, and the life" (John 14:6). The third member of the Godhead, the Comforter, is called the "Spirit of truth."

If we think of only things that are true and honest, we will not consider lying. The Bible says, "A righteous man hateth lying" (Prov. 13:5). For God is a God of truth and lying is an abomination to Him. Therefore it must be thought of in that way by His children, for lies originate in the mind. The Bible says that all liars shall be thrown into the Lake of Fire some day (Rev. 21:8).

According to the Lord Jesus Christ, the devil is the father of lies and liars (John 8:37-45). Jesus actually said that the devil was the father of the Jews who were speaking to Him, even though those Jews were Jesus' kinsmen and as a nation the Jews were considered God's chosen people. But they refused the truth of God and preferred to believe a lie.

Therefore, in line with thinking of whatsoever is true, we have to know and believe what is true. Jesus promised that the Spirit of truth would guide us into all truth. When we open our hearts to God,

His Spirit will help us to know what is true and what is false.

An acquaintance of mine named George was once an atheist. He actively worked at converting others to his viewpoint. He read everything he could get his hands on that supported the atheistic point of view. He felt certain that facts of science could never be reconciled to Biblical teachings. He was an ardent advocate of the evolution theory.

While he was in his first year of graduate school at Syracuse University he was stricken by a mysterious illness. He was hospitalized for several months and none of the doctors could determine what was wrong. God sent a witness to him while he was there. The young man in the bed next to his was a Christian, and also an Ivy-League intellectual type which he admired.

George became curious and started reading the Bible someone had brought to him. One night he became convicted of his sinfulness before God and his need of Christ as Saviour, and he knelt in the darkness by his bed and asked the Lord to save him. Suddenly he understood a lot of things he had never understood before—and he knew that the Bible was the Word of God.

Two days later George was released from the hospital. Much to the amazement of the doctors, his mysterious ailment was gone. George eventually became a professor in the science department of a Christian university and with two fellow professors he holds seminars for young people on Science and the Bible.

Righteous Thinking

Philippians 4:8 also says we are to think on things that are "just." The Greek word for this carries the meaning of equitable or righteous. Following this advice, we will not plan to do anything that is unfair, unjust, or unrighteous.

By thinking equitably about all things, we will not judge unfairly or prematurely, without knowing all the facts; we will stand up for that which is true; and we will be righteous in our dealings with men.

Before Zacchaeus came to Christ, he was a mean, money-grubbing, conniving publican. According to *The Westminster Dictionary of the Bible*, "With a few honorable exceptions, the publicans, great and small, were extortioners."

Yet after Zacchaeus surrendered to the Lord, he said, "Behold, Lord, the half of my goods I give to the poor; and if I have taken any thing from any man by false accusation, I restore him fourfold" (Luke 19:8). Within an hour this man's thinking had switched from "unjust" to "just." In fact, the definition "righteous" for that Greek word fits in even better here, in view of Zacchaeus' bubbling-over desire to restore fourfold!

Pure Thinking

The next word in our verse is "pure," which also means "clean" and "modest." Thinking "pure" automatically excludes impure or "dirty" thinking. This type of thinking has no place at all in the mind of a Christian.

Before I turned my life over to Jesus Christ at the age of 24, I was quite talented at remembering and telling off-color stories. I enjoyed making my friends laugh by using just the right emphasis. But when I came to Christ, those vulgar stories became repugnant to me. They were the first thing of which God convicted me.

Ever since then it has been a puzzle to me how professing Christians can tell suggestive stories. According to the Bible, they can't do this and be right with the Lord. Ephesians 5:4 decries filthiness, foolish talking, and vulgar witticisms. "Out of the abundance of the heart, the mouth speaketh."

Impure thoughts may be sent into our minds by Satan; but they must be rejected instantly and replaced by pure, God-honoring thoughts, which are the antidote. The Biblical prescription for Satanic temptations is James 4:7-8—"Submit yourselves therefore to God. Resist the devil, and he will flee from you. Draw nigh to God, and he will draw nigh to you."

Some professing Christians undoubtedly turn away from the Lord because they have allowed sinful, impure thoughts to dwell in their minds. They have grieved and quenched the Holy Spirit. Sometimes they do the wicked things their imaginations have suggested. The time to stop Satan's rule of our lives is in the thought stage! Once he gets a toehold in the living room, he can take over the whole house.

The Bible says about people who turn from God:

> And even as they did not like to retain God in their knowledge, God gave them over to a reprobate mind, to do those things which are not convenient: being filled with all unrighteousness, fornication, wickedness, covetousness, maliciousness; full of envy, murder, debate, deceit, malignity; whispers, backbiters, haters of God, despiteful, proud, boasters, inventors of evil things, disobedient to parents . . . (Rom. 1:28-30).

Note that the above scripture says that because these people had a "reprobate mind" they did the indecent things that came out of it.

Lovely Thinking

Think on things that are lovely, our verse says. In these days of mad rush, I think many of us miss out on the lovely things of life. They're still all around us, even as they were in the olden, more rural days—but we're often too busy to notice them, aren't we?

Have you ever stopped to look at a tiny weed flower? If not, some day stoop to pick up one of those delicate little yellow, lavendar, or white flowers that may dot your lawn. Imagine God putting all that beauty and workmanship into a little thing like that! ". . . Even Solomon in all his glory was not arrayed like one of these," Jesus said.

Yes, all around us are lovely things to think

about—birds and animals, babies and mothers, waterfalls and sunsets. God's love, answers to prayer, and the kind deeds of others also fall into this category.

Thinking the Best

Think on things that are "of good report." That can include the soul-winning, sacrificial efforts of missionaries and other Christians; the good works that are being done by others; the way God has answered prayer. The opposites are remembering (and passing on) evil gossip; believing the worst of others; mulling over real or imagined wrongs; and worrying about all the dire things that may come to pass.

Some people build themselves up by tearing others down. They are forever finding fault with others. Some of it may be true, while some may be largely imagined—for they may be projecting their own shortcomings on those they criticize. But this critical attitude has its birth in their minds. Yes, it's an attitude, it's a bad habit, a wrong way of thinking that they have developed.

God tells us to think on things that are "of good report," and He also says, "if there be any virtue or any praise." Mix these three together and they provide the perfect antidote for a critical spirit! If we find ourselves thinking of the shortcomings of someone else, let us replace those thoughts with kinder ones. No doubt that person has some attributes worthy of praise. Think on those things.

Jesus said, "Therefore all things whatsoever ye would that men should do to you, do ye even so to them, for this is the Law and the Prophets" (Matt. 7:12). If you would that men would think the best of you, you must think the best of them. Love begets love. If we do feel their lives are not what they ought to be, then we should pray for them. We all can use some prayer, can't we!

We all appreciate being sincerely praised. If you're a woman and you've worked hard to prepare a delicious meal, you like to have someone say so. If you're a man and you've done something well, it makes you feel wonderful to have someone notice. Too often, however, in our families we tend to criticize instead of praise, don't we? This comes straight from the way our minds are set. Are they set for "if there be any virtue, and if there be any praise"?

Morris E. Taylor wrote in an article in "The Lutheran"—"People generally fulfill our expectations. Children who are condemned by their parents generally live down to what is said about them. Wives who are accused of infidelity generally find a way to act out the accusation."

Your thinking can wreck your world and those of others—or it can make a Heaven on earth wherever you are. If you're unhappy and your home life is unpleasant and your co-workers are hard to get along with—it may be that by earnestly applying the principles of thinking set forth in Philippians 4:8, you can change your world!

4
YOUR MENTAL ENVIRONMENT

Hear, O Israel: The Lord our God is one Lord: And thou shalt love the Lord thy God with all thine heart, and with all thy soul, and with all thy might. And these words, which I command thee this day, shall be in thine heart: And thou shalt teach them diligently unto thy children, and shalt talk of them when thou sittest in thine house, and when thou walkest by the way, and when thou liest down, and when thou risest up. And thou shalt bind them for a sign upon thine hand, and they shall be as frontlets between thine eyes. And thou shalt write them upon the posts of thy house, and on thy gates.

—Deuteronomy 6:4-9

Dr. G. Campbell Morgan, the great Christian preacher and writer, wrote in his booklet, "Life's Problems," the following: "It is impossible for any man, whatever his position in the realm of thought may be, to deny that men bequeath to their children their dispositions, their tendencies, their character. . . . Remember you never touch a man without influencing him."

We are constantly being influenced in our thinking by what we see, hear, and experience. Some of this is affected, of course, by our own previously formed opinions. For instance, if one happens to be a dyed-in-the-wool conservative, he probably won't be swayed by liberal appeals. If he is a tee-totaler, a whiskey advertisement will make little impression on him. Nevertheless, anything that enters our consciousness may subtly modify our thinking.

This is why the Lord gave the commands of Deuteronomy 6:4-9 to the Children of Israel. First, their whole beings were to be permeated with love for God. This acts as a barrier against unwholesome, destructive, ungodly thoughts (which in turn would lead to unlawful acts).

Israel was instructed to keep God's Word in their hearts, to teach it to their children, to talk about it in their homes and abroad, day and night. They were told to wear it on their persons and even put scripture texts all over their dwelling places.

Unfortunately the people probably did not obey this command. For if they had, they would never have forgotten God's law or gone after strange gods. The Old Testament is a history of Israel's failure to live up to God's commands and the resultant tragedies that came into their lives because they didn't. In speaking of God's judgment on their failure, the Apostle Paul wrote:

Now all these things happened unto them for en-samples: and they are written for our admonition, upon whom the ends of the world are come. Wherefore let him that thinketh he standeth take heed lest he fall (I Cor. 10:11-12).

Here Paul warns us that we need to be careful lest we fall. And he advises us that we can learn from the Biblical record of Israel's experience.

The Influence of Family and Fellow Believers

When Israel was in the wilderness, the people became discouraged ... "and the people spake against God and against Moses" (Num. 21:5). The fact that they were all together in it indicates that there must have been a great deal of murmuring, complaining, and gossiping going on.

Perhaps to begin with, there were many who were seeking to trust the Lord, as well as their leader Moses. But after allowing the grumblers to fill their ears for awhile, they too became dissatisfied. Their minds were influenced. They joined the growing crowd. "And the Lord sent fiery serpents among the people, and they bit the people; and much people of Israel died" (Num. 21:6).

A grumbling spirit is catching. It is best to avoid grumblers and fault-finders as much as possible; but if unavoidable, then it is God-honoring on our part to change the subject.

For if we listen much to complainers and gossips, we shall tend to become like them. It will spoil our peace and joy and love. Our Christian testimony

43

will be marred. Contentions and factions will disrupt our church and may cause our young people and others to be disillusioned with "Christianity."

The Apostle Paul also wrote to the Corinthians:

> Now I beseech you, brethren, by the name of our Lord Jesus Christ, that ye all speak the same thing, and that there be no divisions among you; but that ye be perfectly joined together in the *same mind* and in the same judgment (1 Cor. 1:10).

That "same mind" would have to be the "mind of Christ" of which Paul spoke in Philippians 2. It would have to be a mind centered on the things mentioned in our original text. It would have to be humble and God-centered.

The Influence of Unbelieving Friends and Associates

Again Israel was led into sin when they became friends with the Moabites at Shittim (Num. 25) ... "and the people began to commit whoredom with the daughters of Moab ... and bowed down to their gods."

Here again their thinking was affected by their companions—only this time they had as friends people who did not know God. While it is true that Christians must live in this world, they need to be constantly on their guard against absorbing its polluted ideas.

44

The wisdom of this world is tainted. The Bible says, "For the wisdom of this world is foolishness with God" (I Cor. 3:19).

The Bible also says, in speaking of people who have turned from God:

> Professing themselves to be wise, they became fools ... wherefore God also gave them up to uncleanness through the lusts of their own hearts, to dishonor their own bodies between themselves: Who changed the truth of God into a lie, and worshipped and served the creature more than the Creator.... And even as they did not like to retain God in their knowledge, God gave them over to a reprobate mind (Rom. 1:22-28).

The Influence of Tainted Wisdom

The wisdom of this world taints the books, magazines, and newspapers we read. It taints the television programs and movies. It taints the teaching in schools and churches. It taints politics and business and international relationships and almost everything.

Our world has gone sex-crazy. No longer do we read the sweet romantic stories of bygone days. There's nothing sweet or good or noble about most of the heroes and heroines of today's literature and plays. That's strictly passé, isn't it?

In South Carolina some years ago a man attacked a teenage couple one Sunday night, chopped off their heads, and threw their bodies into an old well. When policemen investigated the man's dwell-

45

ing place they found piles of horror comic books—from which he had derived his grisly idea.

This man accepted Christ as his Saviour while he was in death row at prison. But it was too late to save the lives of that young couple. Perhaps, if this murderer had been led to Christ earlier in life and had learned to read the Bible instead of those comic books, two people would still be alive today.

Most people are not led to such an extreme as this by what they see and hear—but many are led into more careless thinking, and from that into more careless living.

The late James H. McConkey said:

> For the mind is the vestibule of the heart. Keep out the pitch and the slime of impurity in any shape or form, else it will soon seep down into the heart and become the seed of deadly temptation. All foul and suggestive things which enter the mind are like the streams which feed the river of lust and passion, and unless you shut off these tiny streams the river will overflow its banks in some unguarded hour, and work your moral and spiritual undoing.
>
> —*The Way of Victory*

It's hard to avoid seeing or hearing things that might be detrimental to our thinking; but we can certainly make every effort to do so, can't we? Why should we allow our minds to be degraded? The Bible says, "For to be carnally minded is death; but to be spiritually minded is life and peace" (Rom. 8:6).

Developing the spiritual mind that gives life and peace depends much on the people with whom we spend our time, the places we frequent, the way we use our spare time, the schools and churches we attend. All of these affect our thinking, for good or evil.

Are our best friends devout Christians who love the Lord and are seeking to serve Him? Or are they people who drink and curse and tell off-color jokes? They say you can tell a person by his friends.

Do we love to attend gatherings of our fellow Christians—or do we prefer parties or social clubs where the smoke is so thick you can almost part it with your hand and the highballs get people to act foolishly? Which type of surroundings do you think lead to a life of peace? And which to a life of regret and guilt?

Do we spend time each day in prayer and communion with our God, in reading and studying His Word? Or do we prefer gossiping, looking at television, or reading sexy books and magazines? Is the way we spend our time making us better, happier, more fruitful Christians—or destroying our testimony and degrading our minds?

Do the schools we or our children attend encourage faith in God or destroy it with their teachings? The same might even be asked about our churches. I remember a woman I worked with in New Jersey. She was a Sunday School teacher and faithfully went to her church. But she did not know Christ as her Saviour.

One day she came in to work and said enthusiastically, "Our pastor is conducting a series of Bible studies for the Lenten season, and oh, it's so interesting! He's explaining to us why various portions in the Bible cannot be believed to be true." This lady's faith in God's Word was being systematically destroyed by the very one who should have been building it up.

And I have met others who attended similar churches. A distinguished doctor told me that before he came to know Christ as his Saviour, he and his wife went to a church where the Sunday School literature was anti-Bible, anti-American, and carried the Communistic line. He and his wife were shocked. Satan loves to get his ideologies in where we least expect to find them.

Also, there are religious people who broadcast over the radio or who go from door to door spreading their propaganda. Some Christians listen to them and even contribute to their cause. But in many cases these door-to-door visitors are spreading a false gospel. The Bible says, "Cease, my son, to hear the instruction that causeth to err from the words of knowledge" (Prov. 19:27).

Yes, our hearts can even be led away from our Lord if we listen to the wrong religious teaching. That is why we need to read and know God's Word. The Apostle Paul warned against "false apostles, deceitful workers, transforming themselves into the apostles of Christ" (II Cor. 11:13).

A person who desires to have a sound mind filled with the peace and joy of the Lord will fill his mind with God's Word. He will read it, memorize it, and teach it to others. Above all, he will seek to obey it. He will yield his heart, his will, to God and be filled with the Spirit so that he is enabled to obey it.

In addition to the Bible there are many fine books written by dedicated Christians that can help us in our Christian growth, such as those by D.L. Moody, Ruth Paxson, and James McConkey.

Christ-centered magazines, newspapers, and Sunday School literature can also elevate our thinking—and so can listening to Bible-believing, Christ-honoring preachers and teachers. The Bible says:

> Set your affection [mind, ASV] on things above, not on things on the earth. For ye are dead, and your life is hid with Christ in God. When Christ, who is our life, shall appear, then shall ye also appear with him in glory (Col. 3:2-3).

Do you love God with all your heart, soul, and mind? Are His words in your heart? Do you talk daily about the things of God with your friends and family? Do you teach them to your children? Do the plaques and pictures in your home remind you and others of God and His Word?

According to God's Word, this is the ideal mental environment for people. Are you enjoying it?

5

TWO MINDS— SPIRITUAL AND CARNAL

For to be carnally minded is death; but to be spiritually minded is life and peace.

Romans 8:6

According to God's Word, there are two types of minds—the carnal mind and the spiritual mind. The Bible says that the carnal mind is enmity against God; it is concerned with the things of the flesh. It is egocentric. It is not subject to the law of God (Rom. 8:7).

The spiritual mind is God-centered. It is led and controlled by the Spirit of God. It is dead to self, alive to God. "Christ liveth in me," is its theme. The thoughts of the spiritual mind are for the glory of God.

The Bible says, "Now those who are made of the dust are like him who was first made of the dust— earth-minded; and as is [the Man] from heaven, so also [are those] who are of heaven—heaven-minded" (I Cor. 15:48, Amplified, N.T.).

When a person is born into God's family through repentance of sin and acceptance of Jesus Christ as his Saviour, he receives the "spiritual mind." The

Bible says, "But ye are not in the flesh, but in the Spirit, if so be that the Spirit of God dwell in you. Now if any man have not the Spirit of Christ, he is none of his. And if Christ be in you, the body is dead because of sin; but the Spirit is life because of righteousness" (Rom. 8:7-8).

However, we also have the carnal mind still present after we are saved, because we are still in the flesh. That is why we have such conflict at times in our hearts—it is conflict between the old nature and new nature (Rom .7).

"The mind of man is the battleground on which every moral and spiritual battle is fought," says J. Oswald Sanders. "Because of its inherited bias toward sin, the natural mind is hostile to God and does not submit to God's law—'indeed, it cannot' (Rom. 8:7)."—*A Spiritual Clinic*.

That is why the Apostle Paul wrote to the Ephesians to "put off the old man ... put on the new man" (Eph. 4:22-24). "Now your attitudes and thoughts all must change," he said (Eph. 4:23, Living N.T.).

When we enter the Christian life we are "babes in Christ," as the Corinthian Christians were (I Cor. 3:1). The Apostle Paul chided them for having remained babes in Christ, saying, "For ye are yet carnal; for whereas there is among you envying and strife and divisions, are ye not carnal and walk as men?" (I Cor. 3:3). They had not matured as Christians.

God wants His children to grow in grace and knowledge of the Lord, so that the spiritual mind takes predominance more and more in the life. Unfortunately, however, we can look around us today and see too many "Corinthian Christians" and all to few "Philadelphian Christians." (Philadelphia was the faithful church spoken of in Revelation 3:7.)

The Corinthian church was not only full of envying, strife, and divisions. Some of the members were also lascivious, immoral, lacking in love toward one another, selfish, proud, disorderly, and listening to false teachers. In addition, the Apostle Paul mentioned the possibility of his finding among them debates, wraths, backbitings, whisperings, swellings, and tumults (II Cor. 12:20). Yes, they were quite a crowd!

It's little wonder then that the Apostle Paul urged them, "Examine yourselves, whether ye be in the faith" (II Cor. 13:5). And certainly we, who have more of the Bible than did the Corinthian Christians, need to do likewise if our lives exhibit any of the characteristics that theirs did.

We need to make sure that we have truly repented of our sins and have received Jesus Christ as our personal Saviour—that we have been truly born again of the Holy Spirit. Otherwise, we are still lost in our sins.

The person who grows in the Lord through reading and hearing His Word and spending time with Him develops his spiritual mind as he yields his will to God's. He comes to love God with all his heart. He has great reverence for Him and great faith in Him. He seeks to obey God and all His revealed will. He dies daily to self.

Of which mind are you today—spiritual or

carnal? There is great power and peace in spiritual thinking—but for the carnally minded, there's nothing but trouble!

The Carnal Mind

There are two types of people who might be considered carnal, according to the Bible. There are the unsaved, called "the natural man" (I Cor. 2:14), and those who remain "babes in Christ."

Dr. L. Gilbert Little writes, "The natural, unregenerate man cannot change his thinking, because his thinking is unspiritual; and unspiritual people can think only of self" (*Nervous Christians*).

But when that self is humbled and cries, "God, be merciful to me a sinner, and save me for Jesus' sake," then the Spirit of God comes into the heart. At that moment of abject humility of self, we become the temple of the Holy Spirit (I Cor. 6:19). Enthroned in our hearts, He has our minds also.

However, before very long Satan and self start pushing in again, as Christians in *Pilgrim's Progress* soon found out! And we suddenly may realize that there's this war going on for our minds, for our hearts. Actually Satan and self are on the same side, because if Satan can get us to put self first, then he's in the driver's seat!

Thus the battle commences, and at first and perhaps for quite awhile we seesaw back and forth in our Christian living. We're up one week and down the next. We're serving avidly for awhile and then down in a slump. We rise up on wings like an eagle—and then we fall flat on our faces. We're living in Romans 7. Some Christians never seem to go any further than this. They stay in the Wilderness of Sin and never make it in this life to the Promised Land of Rest!

Self dies so hard! We think we have it licked when up it jumps again. "It is always self who gets irritable and envious and resentful and critical and worried," says Roy Hession in *The Calvary Road.* "It is self who is hard and unyielding in its attitudes toward others. It is self who is shy and self-conscious and reserved. No wonder we need breaking. As long as self is in control, God can do little with us, for all the fruits of the Spirit ... with which God longs to fill us, are the complete antithesis of the hard, unbroken spirit within us and presupposes that it has been crucified."

The "carnal" Christian is frequently found to be a legalist, like the Galatians. That is, he has a little set of rules by which he lives and then is very proud of his "holiness," when in actuality he may be trampling underfoot God's rules for holiness, which can only be obeyed in the Spirit. The Galatians were evidently "biting and devouring one another" and had to be reminded by Paul, "Thou shalt love thy neighbor as thyself" (Gal. 5:14-15). They were trying to achieve perfection, and even salvation, through the works of the law—the efforts of the flesh—rather than by the indwelling Spirit of God. The Apostle Paul wrote to them:

This only would I learn of you, Received ye the Spirit by the works of the law, or by the hearing of faith? Are ye so foolish? Having begun in the Spirit, are ye now made perfect by the flesh? (Gal. 3:2-3).

Andrew Murray said, "One great cause of the feebleness of so much Christian living is because it is more under law than under grace" (*The School of Obedience*).

On the other side of the coin, but still in the "carnal Christian" realm are those who proclaim so vehemently that they are "under grace" that they feel they can disobey some of the plain commands in God's Word! I've heard such a person taking God's holy name in vain more than once; I've heard him continually condemn his fellow Christians; I've seen him in a murderous rage.

"There is much misunderstanding of grace," writes J.F. Strombeck. "Few indeed seem to have grasped its true and full meaning. Grace never means a license to sin, as some seem to think. In fact, it is grace that prevents a believer from sinning" (*Disciplined by Grace*). If a person lacks victory, it's because he lacks grace. And if he lacks grace, it's because he's deficient in obedience. He's not walking with the Lord.

When we walk in the Spirit, we do not habitually break God's laws (I John 3:9). Paul, the Apostle of grace, wrote, "What shall we say then? Shall we continue in sin, that grace may abound? God forbid. How shall we, that are dead to sin, live any longer therein? (Rom. 6:1-2).

The carnal professing Christian claims that he loves God, but often shows by his actions and

55

words how shallow his profession is. It is hard to tell many times whether such a person is saved or not, although he may say that he is. His attitude is apt to be careless rather than reverent. He is usually too busy to spend time with God. He may even be busy "in the Lord's work," but because he's doing it in the energy of the flesh, he doesn't accomplish much.

The carnal Christian is one who grieves the Holy Spirit by sinning, who quenches the Holy Spirit by refusing to listen to Him. No wonder such a one cannot be filled with the Spirit, or walk in the Spirit, or exhibit the fruit of the Spirit!

The growth-arrested "babe in Christ" is an immature Christian. He cannot weather the storms of life as the spiritual Christian does. He may become neurotic, or develop psychosomatic ailments, or even suffer mental illness.

But the good Lord uses these trials the immature Christian brings on himself, as well as those He Himself sends, to bring His child to maturity. If we would allow God to control our heart-minds, we'd save ourselves a lot of trouble and heartache!

The Spiritual Mind

When a person turns from his sin and receives Jesus Christ as his personal Saviour, he receives the same potential as every other new-born babe in Christ. He becomes a new creature, with new aspirations in his heart-mind. Concerning the new covenant ushered in for man by the death of Jesus Christ on the cross, the Bible says:

> This is the covenant that I will make with them after those days, saith the Lord, I will put my laws into their *hearts,* and in their *minds* will I write them; and their sins and iniquities will I remember no more. (Heb. 10:16-17).

Now the secret of living the Christian life is not in striving. That's of the flesh, and we would claim credit for victory, if there were any. No, the secret is in merely *yielding* to the new life, new heart-mind, and new spirit that God has given us! It's a matter of the egocentric will abdicating its throne.

The Holy Spirit will fill our hearts if we will but let Him, and He gives us the power to live a holy life. For "the fruit of the [Holy] Spirit, [the work which His presence within accomplishes]—is love, joy (gladness), faithfulness; (meekness, humility) gentleness, self-control (self-restraint, continence)—Gal. 5:22, *Amplified N.T.* These beautiful qualities can be seen in a spiritually minded Christian.

In his booklet, *The Key to Success in the Christian Life,* Dr. William W. Orr wrote:

> What is the filling of the Spirit? Just what the term implies. It is our lives being filled with Him instead of being filled with ourselves or worldly things. It is to have our new Guest in full possession of every part of our heart. It is having His power surging through you. It is to have His wisdom imbuing your mind.

The Christian walk is not hard if it is done in the Spirit. It's only hard when it's attempted in the flesh. The Apostle Paul wrote:

> For though we walk in the flesh, we do not war after the flesh: (For the weapons of our warfare are not carnal, but mighty through God to the pulling down of strongholds;) casting down imaginations, and every high thing that exalteth itself against the knowledge of God, and bringing into captivity every thought to the obedience of Christ (II Cr. 10:3-5).

The spiritually minded Christian enjoys the peace, joy, comfort, and love of the Lord. He knows his steps are ordered by the Lord. He knows what it is to have the guidance of the Holy Spirit in day-to-day life as well as in important decisions. He sees prayers answered and souls turn to the Lord because of his witness. He experiences power to live a consistent Christian life.

Dr. Robert C. McQuilkin, founder of Columbia Bible College, wrote:

> But walking in the Spirit means more than a standard: it means the provision of God's power to walk according to the standard. If that is so, why are any Christians defeated? Because there is the human responsibility, and this is where Christians fail. We are commanded to walk in the Spirit. We are commanded, "Be filled with the Spirit" (Eph. 5:18). That is, "Live your life in the fullness of the Holy Spirit." There is the choice—the complete committal in surrender and faith.—*Joy and Victory.*

The spiritual man has the love of Christ indwelling him. It was no accident that the Apostle Paul wrote that great chapter on love to those carnal Corinthians!

The ideal for the spiritual Christian is that he be very patient and kind, never jealous or envious, never boastful or proud, never haughty or selfish or rude. He does not demand his own way. He is not irritable or touchy. He does not hold grudges and will hardly even notice when others wrong him. He is never glad about injustice, but rejoices whenever truth wins out (Cp. I Cor. 13:4-6, *Living N.T.*).

The only one who ever measured up perfectly to this ideal was the sinless Lord Jesus. But by the power of the Holy Spirit, each one of us who is born again can come closer to this ideal and thus show forth the lovely Spirit of Christ to all those with whom we come in contact.

It is in our heart-minds where the Holy Spirit works to conform us to the image of Christ. As Evan H. Hopkins wrote in his book, *The Law of Liberty in the Spiritual Life*—"Practical holiness is not something that begins by doing, but by being."

The Importance of Obedience

The first sin that plunged the human race into the abyss of condemnation, death, and estrangement from God was disobedience to God. Thus the perfect, obedient life of our Lord Jesus Christ made it possible for Him to give that life to pay the penalty for our sins and reconcile us to God (Rom. 5:10, 19). Andrew Murray wrote:

> Christ came to show us the nobility, the blessedness, the heavenliness of obedience. When God gave us the robe of creaturehood to wear, we knew not that its beauty, its unspotted purity, was obedience to God. Christ came and put on that robe that He might show us how to wear it, and how with it we could enter into the presence and glory of God. Christ came to overcome, and so bear away our disobedience, and to replace it by His own obedience on us and in us.—*The School of Obedience*.

It is through failure to obey God that most Christians do not become what is called "a victorious Christian." Clinging anxiously to "self," they refuse to yield completely to the Lord. Thus they are not "filled with the Spirit." And it is only through the power of the Holy Spirit that we are able to obey the Lord in all areas of our lives. He produces His fruit in us as we yield.

As one of his ten rules for mental health Dr. Marion H. Nelson gives the following:

> Walk in the light; be obedient to God's laws, no matter what happens (I John 1:7). This, of course, is the way God has indicated that we can avoid damage to our souls by sin in our lives. The Christian who will not agree with God about the sin in his life must reap the consequences. The way of obedience is always the easiest way in the Christian life.—*Why Christians Crack Up*.

I believe it is Satan who makes us think that it's hard to obey God and it's easier to go the way of our carnal inclinations. But disobedience is sin, and sin always leads to trouble and heartache in God's law of sowing and reaping! When we disobey God in word or deed, we ought to have a heart full of sorrow and repentance so that we will not do that thing again! The Bible says:

> For the [true] love of God is this, that we do His commands—keep His ordinances and are *mindful* of His precepts and teaching. And these orders of His are not irksome, burdensome, oppressive or grievous (I John 5:3, *Amplified N.T.*).

It is in God's Word, of course, that we find His will revealed, His commands and principles for godly living. The Bible says that all scripture is "profitable for doctrine, for reproof, for correction, for instruction in righteousness, that the man of God may be perfect, thoroughly furnished unto all good works" (II Tim. 3:16-17).

Of course we need to "rightly divide the word of truth," for certainly the ceremonial laws given the Jews under the old covenant were done away with at the death of Christ (Heb. 10:9-16). But the New Testament as well as the Old is full of rules for godly living which we should obey in the Spirit, because we love God and our fellow man.

Our obedience is not to Law as such, but to Love—to the promptings of the Holy Spirit as He speaks to us in our hearts, through God's Word, through other Christians, and through circumstances.

"But now we are delivered from the law," says the Bible, "that being dead wherein we were held; that we should serve in newness of spirit, and not in the oldness of the letter" (Rom. 7:6).

Note, we are still to serve, but by the Spirit.

Our salvation does not depend upon our obedience to God (except insofar as we obeyed the Gospel and received Christ as Saviour). But if we are truly saved, we will have a desire in our hearts to do God's will. The Bible says, "For it is God which worketh in you both to will and to do of his good pleasure" (Phil. 2:13).

In his *Institutes of the Christian Religion* John Calvin said:

> . . . The pious mind dreams not of any imaginary deity, but contemplates only the one true God. . . . Knowing him to be his Lord and Father, he concludes that he ought to mark his government in all things, revere his majesty, endeavour to promote his glory, and obey his commands.

The Bible points out that "Abraham believed God and it was imputed unto him for righteousness." But in the same passage of scripture James shows how Abraham's faith was evidenced by his works (James 2:20-23). Thus it is only by our life of obedience to God that others can tell that we have truly accepted Jesus Christ as our Saviour and are His followers.

"Thank God that though you once chose to be slaves of sin, now you are obeying with all your heart the teaching to which God has committed you," the Apostle Paul wrote to the Romans. "And now you are free from your old master, sin; and you have become slaves to your new master, goodness and righteousness" (Rom. 6:17-18, *Living Letters*).

And the Lord Jesus said, "He that hath my commandments and keepeth them, he it is that loveth me: and he that loveth me shall be loved of my Father, and I will love him and will manifest myself to him" (John 14:21).

Put On ... Put Off

Perhaps the most outstanding passage in the Bible concerning the old man and the new man is to be found in Ephesians 4 and 5. Paul wrote:

> ... You must stop living as the heathen usually do, in the frivolity of their minds, with *darkened understanding*, estranged from the life of God because of the ignorance that exists among them and because of the stubbornness of their *hearts* (Eph. 4:17-18, *Williams N.T.*).

The unsaved person's mind is frivolous because his understanding is darkened. But when we know Christ as our Saviour, we have the light of God shed abroad in our hearts. Our lives should be entirely different from those in the world around us. We are in the world—but not of it! We're a set-apart people. We are God's children.

So God tells us by Paul to "put off ... the old man, which is corrupt according to deceitful lusts; and be renewed in the spirit of your *mind*" (Eph.

4:22-23). We are to put off lying, wrath, stealing, bitterness, clamour, evil speaking, malice, fornication, uncleanness, covetousness, filthiness, foolish talk, and coarse jesting. In Colossians 3:8-9 we are also told to put off such things.

Putting off the old man is one determined action we are to take, and putting on the new man is the other. According to Paul we are to love one another, forgive one another, be kind and tenderhearted toward one another. We are to prove what is acceptable to the Lord, walk wisely, and redeem the time. We are to be thankful to God and submissive to one another. (See Eph. 4 and 5.) Colossians 3:12-15 says:

> Put on therefore, as the elect of God, holy and beloved, bowels of mercies, kindness, humbleness of mind, meekness, longsuffering; forbearing one another and forgiving one another ... and above all these things put on love, which is the bond of perfectness. And let the peace of God rule in your hearts.

When we come to Christ, we are to throw away our old self-righteous rags (Isa. 64:6), and with them all the ungodly ways of our old life. We are like beggars who have suddenly been adopted by a King. He has a beautiful new white garment for us, of His Son's righteousness; and the ornaments thereof are love, humility, gentleness—and all of the other fruit of the blessed Holy Spirit of God (Gal. 5:22-23).

There are many ways in which the new man is to be different from the old man. He is to keep things

64

right between himself and God (I John 1:9); love not the world (I John 2:15); be separated from the world (II Cor. 6:14-18); love his fellow Christians (I John 4:21); keep his body under (I Cor. 9:27); avoid strife and arguments (II Tim. 2:23); set his mind on things above, not things on earth (Col. 3:2, ASV); do all to the glory of God (I Cor. 10:31).

Death to Self

"I am crucified with Christ—nevertheless I live," wrote Paul, "yet not I, but Christ liveth in me. And the life which I now live in the flesh I live by the faith of the Son of God, who loved me and gave himself for me" (Gal. 2:20).

According to Paul, the old man in all of us who have received Christ as Saviour "is crucified with him." Thus we are freed from the power of sin in our flesh. But as Andrew Murray said, "... The flesh in which I yet am, the old man that was crucified with Him, remained condemned to an accursed death, but is not yet dead."—*Like Christ*.

Here is where the reckoning of Romans 6:11-14 comes in. The Bible says:

Likewise reckon ye also yourselves to be dead indeed unto sin, but alive unto God through Jesus Christ our Lord. Let not sin therefore reign in your mortal body, that ye should obey it in the lusts thereof. Neither yield ye your members as instruments of unrighteousness unto sin; but yield yourselves unto God, as those that are alive

65

from the dead, and your members as instruments of righteousness unto God. For sin shall not have dominion over you: for ye are not under the law, but under grace.

The word "reckon" indicates that the mind is involved in this process. The word used in this text stems from the Greek word "logos," which means among other things, "reasoning" or the mental process. I think this is an attitude of mind that God would have every Christian assume, an attitude that dominates his every waking thought and action.

Back in the first chapter of this book we discussed the truth that as a man thinketh, so is he. If we consider ourselves dead to sin, but alive to God, the only thing that will count in our lives is living to please Him. Our pride will no longer be important; we will abase ourselves that He may have glory. Praise and thankfulness to Him will lift our hearts in song day and night.

Madame Guyon, a woman of God in 17th century France, was persecuted, lied about, and imprisoned. But she rejoiced continually in the Lord. She knew what it was to die daily to self and be alive to God—and she learned it in the "school of hard knocks." The more she tried to live unto God, the harder people made it for her—and conversely, the easier it was for her to live unto God!

Living for self is most unsatisfying. While it may gratify a desire of the moment, it leaves an emptiness in the heart. Jesus set the criterion for the true Christian when He said, "If any man will come after me, let him deny himself, and take up his cross and follow me. For whosoever will save his life shall lose it; and whosoever will lose his life for my sake shall find it" (Matt. 16:24-25).

The most thrilling life in all the world is to be found in living for Jesus.

6
FAITH VERSUS FEAR

*I sought the Lord and he heard me and
delivered me from all my fears.*

Psalm 34:4

Faith and fear are opposite states of mind. If one
of these states is controlling your thinking at a specific time, then the other is not. Which of these
two rules your thought life most of the time?
Whichever has the predominance no doubt also in-
fluences most of your decisions and actions.

Only an attitude of faith can help us to live a
victorious life—a life that is happy and pleasing to
God. Only faith can protect us from the unpleasant
harvest fear produces.

Faith, as spoken of in the New Testament, is
"that leaning of the entire human personality on
God in absolute trust and confidence in His power,
wisdom, and goodness," according to Alexander
Souter's *Pocket Lexicon to the Greek New Testament*. Is that the state of mind that you enjoy? If
it is not, then this chapter is especially for you.

Fear, on the other hand, is defined by Webster as
being a painful emotion marked by alarm. It is

anxious anticipation of danger, pain, or something else. It is anxiety, worry, or concern. Fear is one of the first basic emotions of a baby, and it performs a valuable service to human beings when allowed to function correctly. It protects them from getting into dangerous situations; it protects them from death or harm.

However, in too many cases the kind of fear we're talking about denotes a lack of trust in God, doesn't it? For if a person has absolute faith in the Lord, he will trust and not be afraid. He will pray and not be anxious. Faith and fear cannot abide side by side.

Actually when faith is ruling, it is through a person's heart—his innermost being, his intellect, his mind. When fear is ruling, a person's emotions control his thinking. Some Bible expositors hold that our emotions are part of our hearts, our innermost beings. But when they are in control, a person's thinking is not as rational as it should be, and he is much more apt to make mistakes in judgment.

"Now, the truth is, that this life is not to be lived in the emotions at all, but in the will," Hannah Whitall Smith wrote. "And therefore, if only the will is kept steadfastly abiding in its center, God's will, the varying states of emotion do not the least disturb or affect the reality of life."—*The Christian's Secret of a Happy Life.*

Instead of labeling their patients' problems "mental," as in the past, many psychiatrists now call some of these problems "emotional." And I feel that the Lord has given me the following enlightenment on this: that on the basis of II Tim-

69

othy 1:7 and the findings of psychologists on the emotion of fear, I believe that fear or sin is at the bottom of perhaps all of the problems which psychiatrists label "emotional."

"For God hath not given us the spirit of fear," says II Timothy 1:7, "but of power, and of love, and of a sound mind." Note that "a sound mind" is the opposite of a "spirit of fear." Such a mind needs no psychiatrist!

In studying the effects of the emotion of fear on men who had engaged in aerial combat, psychologists reported the following physical symptoms: irritability, butterflies in stomach, feeling of unreality, feeling confused and rattled, poor memory for what happened on mission, poor ability to concentrate, restlessness, feeling tired out, feeling depressed, grouchiness, poor appetite, and bad dreams. (Ernest R. Hilgard, *Introduction to Psychology*, page 120.)

Fear can lead to an unbalanced mind. It is certainly the basis for feelings of insecurity, inferiority complex, anxiety, obsession, and compulsion.

But God has provided us with the power to cast out all fear from our hearts. And that power is to be found in *faith*. And that faith must be in God's love for us. For the Bible says, "There is no fear in love, but perfect love casteth out fear: because fear hath torment. He that feareth is not made perfect in love. We love him, because He first loved us" (I John 4:18-19).

Have you ever stopped to consider how many things we take by faith each day? We have absolute confidence that the alarm clock will wake us up at the right time. We doubt not a bit that the school bus will come by at a certain time to pick up the children. We know that the office will still be where we left it the night before. We believe so much that we'll get our pay check on a certain day that we have more than half of it spent before we get it!

We take for granted that the earth, sun, moon, and stars will stay in their courses. Yet for some reason we can't bring ourselves to trust absolutely the One Who put them there and keeps them there.

The Lord Jesus Christ, by Whom all things were made, said to His disciples, "Why are ye fearful, O ye of little faith?" Although their position seemed perilous—their small ship was about to sink in the terrible Galilean storm—Jesus rebuked them for their fear and little faith.

Yes, it's true that He was with them at the time. But actually isn't it also true that He is with every one of us who knows Him as our Saviour? What then have we to fear?

The Object and Source of Faith

The object and source of faith is God, for He alone can help us. In order to have His help, however, we have to be in a right relationship with Him. The Lord Jesus Christ, God's Son, said, "I am the way, the truth, and the life; no man cometh unto the Father but by Me" (John 14:6).

God sent His Son into the world to reconcile us to Himself. But in order to be reconciled to God, we have to accept by faith the gift of salvation He offers us. The Bible says, "For by grace are ye saved through faith; and that not of yourselves: it is the gift of God: Not of works, lest any man should boast" (Eph. 2:8-9).

It is by faith then that we accept the fact that we can do nothing to save ourselves. It is by faith that we receive the Lord Jesus Christ as our personal Saviour and acknowledge that "we have redemption through His blood, the forgiveness of sins, according to the riches of His grace" (Eph. 1:7). The wisdom of this world mocks at the blood of Jesus Christ and seeks to eliminate it—but faith takes God's Word for it that it's the only way to be saved.

Many people stumble at the Gospel because they try to approach it by logic, when it can only be approached by simple, childlike faith. The Lord Jesus said, "Verily I say unto you, Whosoever shall not receive the kingdom of God as a little child, he shall not enter therein" (Mark 10:15).

Faith accepts the miraculous virgin birth of the Son of God. Faith acknowledges His perfect life, His teachings, and His miracles. Faith believes that Jesus Christ died on the cross for sinners, that He arose from the grave, that He ascended into Heaven, and that He now sits on the right hand of God interceding for those who love Him.

Faith looks forward to His imminent return. Faith believes God's Holy Word. Faith rejoices in opportunities in which to exercise itself! Faith gives peace and confidence in the midst of raging storms of life.

Fear, Worry, Anxiety

Because it has had so much practical influence in my life, one of my favorite passages of scripture is the following:

> Be anxious about nothing, but in everything by prayer and supplication with thanksgiving let your requests be made known unto God. And the peace of God, which passeth all understanding, shall keep your hearts and minds through Christ Jesus (Phil. 4:6-7).

Fairly early in my Christian life I had the joy of learning how to apply these verses to daily living. My husband was out of work, we had a new car and house on which to meet payments—and I had the abominable luck to run into a lawyer's car with that new car of ours! I was worrying myself sick. But then the second part of the above verse was used in a benediction at my church.

When I got home I looked the scripture up to find out more about how the peace of God could keep my heart and mind through Christ Jesus. And I found that the secret lay in my bringing every concern, little and big, to my Lord—and not being anxious about it, because He could take care of it. The thanksgiving is important too, for as we thank the Lord for the way in which He helped us in the past, it fills our hearts with faith that He will do so now and in the future.

As I prayed, the Lord led me to call the lawyer

and tell him our situation. He settled for $20. My husband got a job through a member of our church, and I also found a part-time job. Thus the Lord met our needs. And I know from long experience that, as we look to Him, the Lord guides and helps us in every problem.

In his book, *Release From Tension*, Dr. Paul E. Adolph writes;

> Anxiety and worry represent forms of fear which project themselves into the future and often concern themselves with imaginary situations which never come to pass. Indeed, it often happens when the future situation arrives, it is devoid of all the contemplated elements which are anticipated.

Mark Twain said, "I am an old man and have known many troubles, but most of them never happened." And psychologists say that 90% of the things people worry about never come to pass. Yet often we spend our time needlessly fretting about things, don't we? Wouldn't it be far better to take the whole 100% to the Lord and trust His hand to be on the 10% that may come to pass?

In speaking of illness, for instance, and how our fretting can bring it on, Dr. Adolph says, "The very thing you feared—sickness—comes, not because your body is worn out, but simply because that collection of fears has reached the point where it can no longer be contained."

Fear, worry, and anxiety are not only useless—for they accomplish nothing—but they also bring on us all sorts of additional woes. They make us sick, miserable, and hard to get along with. And they cause us to sin in other ways. For when these are reigning in our hearts instead of faith in God, then we are not walking with the Lord the way we should.

Erich Sauer says in his book, *In the Arena of Faith,* that cares and worries are useless, injurious, unworthy, unfilial, earthly, idolatrous, and heathenish. "All worrying is undignified," he writes. "He who worries is forgetting his high calling, as well as the willingness and power of our great God to help. He is forgetting God's all-sufficiency and perfect wisdom as well as His eternal love."

Charles H. Spurgeon said, "Do not please the devil by distrusting your faithful God."

Basically, worry and anxiety reside in our heart-minds, for these words are descriptive of the thoughts we may be entertaining. The only way to get rid of worry and anxiety is to go to the Lord and allow Him to relieve us and fill our heart-minds with faith.

A number of years ago I was visiting a friend of mine in New Jersey. One afternoon she seemed most distressed. "What's the matter, Ellen*?" I asked. "Can I be of any help?"

"No," she answered, "I don't know if anything can help. I'm so concerned about that boy of mine. He just can't seem to make it at school. Sometimes I think I'll go out of my mind worrying about him!"

I put my arm around her and said, "The Lord

*Fictitious name.

doesn't want His children to fret so about things, Ellen. Have you taken this problem to Him?"

"Oh, of course I have! But I'm still worried sick!"

"Well, when you took the problem to Him, did you leave it with Him?" I asked. "Or when you rose from your knees, did you still carry it on your back?"

Ellen's face lit up with understanding. "I see what you mean!" she exclaimed. "Pray with me, will you, right now?"

Together we knelt by her couch—and when we arose, Ellen's face was serene. "I left it with Him, Muriel—and I feel so much better now!" Years later Ellen told me that that day was the beginning of a new way of life for her—one of taking her burdens to the Lord and trusting to Him for their disposal.

Her son attended a Bible institute when he grew up. He met a lovely Christian girl there whom he married, and he is now a faithful servant of the Lord's.

We live a life of faith when we trust fully in the Lord in every circumstance. We need not fear that we'll make the wrong move if we're leaning on the Lord, for God works in us both to will and to do of His good pleasure (Phil. 2:13).

The Bible says, "Cast every worry you have upon Him, because He cares for you" (I Pet. 5:7, *Williams N.T.*).

Trials and Tribulations

Every human being under the sun has his share of troubles and problems. But the Christian has the joy and comfort of knowing that God will work them out for his good (Rom. 8:28). If the Christian truly believes this in his heart, then he becomes a testimony to others of the grace of God when he is undergoing some great trial.

Henry G. Bosch wrote in *Our Daily Bread*, "When God puts a tear in your eye, it's because He wants to put a rainbow in your heart!"

Rev. Richard Wurmbrand, who was tortured for Christ for 14 years in Communist prisons, has told about how some Communists have come to Christ because of the radiant testimonies of those they had tortured. If our fellow Christians can maintain such wonderful faith in their Lord though they are torn from their families and separated for years, though they are unjustly imprisoned and terribly tormented, why then can't we?

After 14 years of suffering and torture Rev. Wurmbrand loves the Lord and the lost souls of Communists more than ever. This is because of an attitude of mind that acknowledges that whatever the Lord permits will work out for good in the end—that it will work out for our good (for the development of a holy character in us); that it will work out for the good of others (for their salvation or for an example to them); and that it will work out for God's glory.

The Lord permits and even sends trials and troubles into our lives so that we may become more like Him, for we are His children. The Bible says He chastens us "for our profit, that we might be partakers of His holiness. Now no chastening for the present seemeth to be joyous, but grievous: nevertheless afterward it yieldeth the peaceable fruit of righteousness unto them which are exercised thereby" (Heb. 12:10-11).

Only by going through the vale of affliction can we acquire that wonderful, promised "peaceable fruit of righteousness." The trials help kill "the old man" in us, as they pull to the fore "the new man." It's grievous for the time, as the Bible says—but it's worth it all! Oh, the sweetness to be found in walking with the Lord, to experience His grace day by day!

An attitude of faith greatly eases the burdens. The Apostle Paul had a heart full of faith, for he wrote, "We are troubled on every side, yet not distressed; we are perplexed, but not in despair; persecuted, but not forsaken; cast down, but not destroyed . . ." (II Cor. 4:8-9).

All God's testings have a purpose—
Someday you will see the light.
All He asks is that you trust Him,
Walk by faith and not by sight.
                                        —Zoller.

The late Dr. Bob Jones, Sr., founder of Bob Jones University, said, "A man is a fool who leans on the arm of flesh when he can be supported by the arm of Omnipotence."

"Trust in the Lord with all thine heart, and lean not unto thine own understanding," says Proverbs 3:5-6. "In all thy ways acknowledge Him, and He shall direct thy paths."

Here again the Bible speaks in terms of our hearts, our innermost beings, our minds—and our understandings. Though we may not understand everything that comes to pass in our lives—and we certainly will not—by trusting in the Lord with all our hearts we will be saved much anxiety. Here also we find another promise from God that if we acknowledge Him in all our ways, He will direct our paths.

In his book, *Nervous Christians*, Dr. L. Gilbert Little writes:

> Worldly Christians, not willing to yield self to the Lord, willfully deceive themselves into believing that the fearful thoughts can be controlled by the will. When this fails (which it always does), they turn to worldly methods and sedatives to divert the thinking processes. The sedatives calm and soothe; the diversions distract the mind; the shock treatments make them forget the symptoms; but none of these therapies deliver them from the source of their suffering, which is the sick soul.

The soul gets sick when it fails to obey God, His Word, and His will. A person may seem to be perfectly all right with God to those with whom he associates casually, for most of us can put on a good front. But those who know him intimately will be aware that something is wrong; for his actions, words, and nervousness will betray him.

The problem is that he isn't fully depending on the Lord because he isn't fully yielded to the Lord. It's hard for a person to trust that the Lord will work all things out for good when that person isn't walking with the Lord. On the other hand, there are times when all of us fail under the weight of pressure, for we are still in the flesh! But if we're trusting in the Lord, we won't stay down.

Psalm 34, that great psalm of deliverance, says:

> What man is he that desireth life and loveth many days, that he may see good? Keep thy tongue from evil and thy lips from speaking guile. Depart from evil and do good; seek peace and pursue it. The eyes of the Lord are upon the righteous, and his ears are open unto their cry ... The Lord is nigh unto them that are of a broken heart; and saveth such as be of a contrite spirit. Many are the afflictions of the righteous: but the Lord delivereth him out of them all (Psa. 34:12-19).

Faith is part of the Christian's armor that protects him from the attacks of Satan. God calls it the shield, and the shield is that which protects one's heart. With the shield of faith one is able to quench all the fiery darts of the wicked one (Eph. 6:16).

India's forest rangers had a rule of conduct to use when they came face to face unexpectantly with a tiger: "Never panic; stare the beast down." Satan, who is likened in the Bible to a roaring lion, may be considered even a more dangerous enemy. But He that is within us is greater than Satan. Therefore with God's shield of faith before us, we can stare the roaring lion down! When we draw nigh to God, and resist the devil, he will flee from us.

Dr. Marion H. Nelson says:

> Please remember that, no matter what the problem is, whether the lies of Satan or physical illness, the peace of mind of the Christian can remain safe from attack, "guarded" so to speak, if the Christian will turn the problem over to God in prayer and leave the problem in God's hands and rest his confidence in God's promises.... God does guard our hearts and minds with His peace, but only when we truly trust Him to handle every problem that comes.—*Why Christians Crack Up.*

God Cares, Comforts, and Provides

How often have we repeated or read, "The Lord is my shepherd; I shall not want"? Dr. Charles L. Allen said in his best-selling book, *God's Psychiatry*, that he prescribed the daily reading of the Twenty-third Psalm to many people who were nervous, tense, worried, and sick—not just once a day, but five times a day. He maintained, "It can change your life in seven days."

Certainly a continual reminder of God's love, care, and provision for us strengthens our faith and helps to banish fears that tie us up in knots. Carl Jung, the well-known Swiss psychiatrist, used to recommend to his patients the singing of "What a Friend We have in Jesus."

Such a recommendation has a good Biblical basis, for the Bible says, "Speaking to yourselves in psalms and hymns and spiritual songs, singing and making melody in your heart to the Lord" (Eph. 5:19). When the heart-mind is thus fortified, fears subside and faith predominates.

Thus the Word of God and Spirit-inspired writings and songs can be great sources of comfort and encouragement if we will allow them that ministry in our lives. Dr. Clyde M. Narramore wrote, "The Christian who is afraid must turn his thoughts back to Calvary and get a fresh vision of Christ's redemptive love for him. He must meditate, moment by moment, on what Christ did and how He overcame for him."—*This Way to Happiness.*

I think one of the greatest passages in the Bible that assures us of the Lord's tender and understanding concern for us is Hebrews 4:15-16:

> For we have not an high priest which cannot be touched with the feeling of our infirmities; but was in all points tempted like as we are, yet without sin. Let us therefore come boldly unto the throne of grace, that we may obtain mercy, and find grace to help in time of need.

How many Christians live in a state of anxiety when God's comfort and reassurance can be had for the asking! In his book, *Grace Abounding to the Chief of Sinners*, John Bunyan told of the fear that came into his heart when he was first imprisoned for preaching the Gospel. He thought sure that he was going to be put to death. But by remembering God's Word and the many examples in it of God's care and love for His people, John came through with a heart full of comfort, which banished the fear and anxiety.

He had also been concerned for the welfare of his wife and children, but then he realized that "if I should venture all for God, then I would be hiring God to take care of all my concerns." He came to the conclusion that his family was actually safer in God's care as long as he was obeying God than they would be in his own care if he were disobeying God.

There in prison Bunyan came to an experiential knowledge of II Corinthians 1:3-5 which says:

> Blessed be God, even the Father of our Lord Jesus Christ, the Father of mercies, and the God of all comfort; Who comforteth us in all our tribulation, that we may be able to comfort them which are in any trouble, by the comfort wherewith we ourselves are comforted of God. For as the sufferings of Christ abound in us, so our consolation also aboundeth by Christ.

God did provide for all the needs of Bunyan's family too, even though the breadwinner of the family was in prison for twelve years off and on! And many Christians can testify how the Lord has met their needs in often miraculous ways.

To me a most precious faith in God's provision has been exemplified by the many married couples I have known who have stepped out in faith to go to a Christian school to prepare for God's service. I know of one couple with three children who did this. By the time they were finished with their training and went out to the mission field they had five children. But God provided for their every need and they've now been serving Him as missionaries for a number of years in India.

The Bible says, "But my God shall supply all your need according to his riches in glory by Christ Jesus" (Phil. 4:19).

Faith Brings Peace and Joy

The Bible also says, "Thou wilt keep him in perfect peace whose mind is stayed on thee: because he trusteth in thee" (Isa. 26:3). Here is another of the many verses in the Bible that tells of the power of right thinking. The epitome of right thinking is the centering of our minds on God, His faithfulness, His love, and His Word. This right thinking taps the power of God to keep us in perfect peace. What a promise!

The Apostle Paul wrote to the Romans, "May the hope-inspiring God so fill you with perfect joy and peace through your continuing faith, that you may bubble over with hope by the power of the Holy Spirit" (Rom. 15:13, *Williams N.T.*).

Paul, as well as his partner Silas, exhibited joy, peace, faith, and hope when their backs were beaten to ribbons and they were thrown into the Philippian jail. With their feet fastened securely in stocks. The Bible says, "At midnight Paul and Silas prayed and sang praises unto God" (Acts 16:25). No wonder the Lord delivered them in such a mighty way!

"For I know whom I have believed," Paul wrote triumphantly, "and am persuaded that he is able to keep that which I have committed unto him against that day" (II Tim. 1:12).

Believing is a form of thinking—the acceptance of the mind of a concept or truth. Believing the precious promises in God's Word that He will keep us, watch over us, and provide for our every need is powerful right thinking—for God works in response to our faith even as He worked in response to the faith of Paul and Silas. In God's sight every one of His children is just as precious to Him as the greatest saint!

"The Lord is my light and my salvation; whom shall I fear? The Lord is the strength of my life; of whom shall I be afraid?" (Psa. 27:1).

7
LOVE VERSUS HATE

*Hatred stirreth up strifes: but love cov-
ereth all sins.*

—Proverbs 10:12

Without doubt among all the feelings that man en-
tertains in his heart, hostility does the most harm
to him mentally, physically, and spiritually. That is
one reason why Jesus urged His followers to "Love
your enemies, bless them that curse you, do good
to them that hate you and pray for them which
despitefully use you and persecute you" (Matt.
5:44).

Love is the antidote for hate. Love is of God—it
is one of His outstanding attributes. The Bible
says, "He that loveth not knoweth not God; for
God is love" (I John 4:8). God gave His Son to
die for us because of His great love.

Love is a distinguishing characteristic of a Christian. The Apostle John also wrote, "Beloved, let us
love one another: for love is of God. And everyone
that loveth is born of God and knoweth God" (I
John 4:7). The Christian is a child of God and
partakes of His characteristics—or should!

On the other hand, hatred or hostility is a characteristic of Satan. Jesus said to some unbelieving Jews, who were full of hatred toward Him and wanted to kill Him, "Ye are of your father the devil, and the lusts of your father ye will do. He was a murderer from the beginning ..." (Matt. 8:44). Murder, of course, is a manifestation of hostility.

I John 3:12 enlarges on this by explaining Cain's actions—"And be not like Cain who [took his nature and got his motivation] from the evil one and slew his brother. And why did he slay him? Because his deeds were wicked and malicious and his brother's were righteous" (*Amplified N.T.*).

Hostility, then, flows from a sinful heart. Wherever we find bitterness, wrath, envy, anger, clamour, malice, and jealousy, there is sin. The person who has these things in his heart toward others is not right with God—he cannot be right with God. For God is love!

Ephesians 5:31 indicates that the entertainment of such feelings by a Christian grieves the Holy Spirit of God. Such a person cannot be fruitful for God. Nor can he exhibit the fruits of the Spirit. Therefore he cannot enjoy or know love, peace, joy, faith, and the other attributes listed in Galatians 5:22-23.

How many professing Christians are limping along in such a joyless existence? If they are Christians, they cannot be happy while thus estranged from their Father in Heaven.

As long as a person nourishes sinful attitudes in his heart, he will not only be miserable but make others miserable as well. The Bible says of such a person, "Forwardness in his *heart*, he *deviseth* mischief continually; he *soweth* discord" (Prov. 6:14). Here is the heart-mind-action relationship verified in God's Word.

Love for God

The more we love God, the more we will want to be like Him. The more we love God and want to please Him, the more we will have the power to do so. For the Holy Spirit only fills us insofar as we yield ourselves to God.

F.B. Meyer in his book, *Five Musts of the Christian Life*, tells the following:

> When the wife of Tigranes came out of the pavilion of Alexander the Great, they asked her what she thought of the costly adorning and furniture of the interior, and she replied that she had no eyes, except for the man—her husband—who had willingly offered to die if she might be spared.

This is the same kind of love and devotion we ought to have for God our Saviour. For the Bible tells us, "Herein is love, not that we loved God, but that He loved us, and sent His Son to be the propitiation for our sins" (I John 4:10).

How can our hearts fail to be filled with gratitude to our Lord for His great sacrifice of love? Perhaps it is because we get so busy in our daily affairs that we tend to forget what God did for us!

Gardiner Spring says:

Among the most convincing of [evidence of the new birth] is love of God. Love to God involves a conviction of His excellence, an inner contentment towards the revelation of his nature, a kindly disposition toward his interest, and gratitude for His favors. The man who possesses this sublime affection has reason to believe that his character differs from what it was by nature.— *The Distinguishing Traits of Christian Character*.

In many Gospel-preaching churches "revivals" are held periodically. Frequently Christians come forward with tears streaming down their face "to get right with God." They had forgotten their first love, just as the people at Ephesus had. They had slipped back into shortcomings. They had come to take their salvation and their God for granted.

Satan had slipped them a pacifier and they were too full of leaves (outward show) and too barren in their relationship with God to bear any fruit for Him. But through His messenger God whispered to them, "Remember therefore from whence thou art fallen and repent, and do the first works ..." (Rev. 2:5). And in coming back to Him and remembering what He did for them because of His great love, their love and dedication are and they become fruitful once again.

The Bible says, "... The love of God is shed abroad in our hearts by the Holy Spirit which is given unto us" (Rom. 5:5).

Love for the Brethren

The Bible also says, "If a man says, I love God, and hateth his brother, he is a liar: for he that loveth not his brother whom he hath seen, how can he love God whom he hath not seen?" (I John 4:20).

Many people declare that they do love their brothers. But if they slander, gossip, criticize, backbite, judge, envy, bear grudges, fail to forgive, seek to "get even"—is that love? Perhaps we just don't realize that when we do these things, we are revealing a hostility in our hearts, not love! In order to overcome hostility, we need to become aware of it, don't we? We need to catch ourselves when we exhibit these telltale signs!

You know, I think we all need to read I Corinthians 13 frequently. For we all tend to forget; we tend to slip. And Satan has a nasty way of impinging his hostile ideas on our minds, so that we fail as Christians.

Living Letters renders I Corinthians 13:4-6 as follows:

> Love is very patient and kind, never jealous or envious, never boastful nor proud, never haughty nor selfish nor rude. Love does not demand its own way. It is not irritable or touchy. It does not hold grudges and will hardly even notice when others do it wrong. It is never glad about injustice, but rejoices whenever truth wins out.

All of the above-mentioned virtues or shortcomings originate in our hearts, and allowing the love of God to reign in these hearts of ours will cause the virtues to triumph and the shortcomings to be banished. We may be tremendously blessed with talents—but if we lack love, we're nothing!

Love Helps Us to Obey God

The Apostle John wrote, "And this is His commandment, That we should believe on the name of His Son Jesus Christ, and love one another, as He gave us commandment" (I John 3:23). If we believe in God's Son Jesus Christ, we will love God (I John 4:19). And if we love one another, we will not want to hurt one another in any way. Thus we will want to follow the many principles set down in God's Word for godly living.

Long ago an unknown writer paraphrased the ten commandments in the following way:

Love to God will admit no other God.
Love resents everything that debases its object by representing it by an image.
Love to God will never dishonor His name.
Love to God will reverence His day.
Love to parents makes one honor them.
Hate, not love, is a murderer.
Lust, not love, commits adultery.
Love will give, but never steal.
Love will not slander or lie.
Love's eye is not covetous.

91

Thus love enables us to obey God—for love fulfills all the law (Gal. 5:14). John wrote in his second epistle, "And this is love, that we walk after His commandments" (II John 6). If we can grasp this first principle of love with all our hearts, minds, and souls, then living a holy life for God won't be hard at all.

One Thing We Should Hate

There is only one thing that God would have us hate—one thing toward which we should definitely feel hostile—and that is sin. Gardiner Spring says:

> The leading thought which influences the soul in all godly sorrow is the intrinsic vileness of sin. It is not enough to feel and acknowledge that we are sinners; the mind must be imbued with a deep and settled conviction of the great evil of sin as committed against God, and as a wanton and wicked violation of His most holy law.—*The Distinguishing Traits of Christian Character.*

The more we love God, the more we will hate sin—for it is the only thing that He hates! "Abhor that which is evil," the Bible says. And as we abhor the sin in ourselves, our minds will reject sinful thoughts and behaviour. This abhorrence and rejection of sin which results from our love and dedication to God gives us the power to live righteously and victoriously as Christians should.

Barbara D.* was a dedicated Christian, but she

was married to a professing Christian man who frequently manhandled her and used profanity. It grieved her to hear such language. But after frequent exposure to it, she reasoned, "Perhaps if he hears me use it, he'll stop." Soon she found herself using profanity at times of great stress. She became deeply convicted, but couldn't seem to gain victory over the habit.

One day, however, when her husband was manhandling and cursing her, she broke under the strain. She pulled loose from her husband and walked through the house screaming his foul words hysterically, "I'm not a +%@*&+ . . .!"

It was summer and the windows were open. Across the street in her front yard was a neighbor whose child had come to Barbara's Bible Club. The next time Barbara held a Bible club this child as well as many others in the neighborhood did not attend. Barbara realized what had happened and wept bitter tears before the Lord. She had lost her testimony. She turned in utter abhorrence from the sin of using foul and profane language. After that she had victory.

Hostility can Wreck Lives

Mildred G.* was a professing Christian who was active in her church. Her husband was a member of the church board. But her heart was full of hostility toward others, especially the new pastor of church. Instead of being special friends with Mil-

*Fictitious name.

dred and her husband as had the former pastor, this minister stepped all over their toes with his messages.

"You're not supposed to preach at us spiritual Christians!" she exclaimed angrily to the pastor one day. "You're supposed to preach to the lost and the carnal!"

When the minister continued with the same type of preaching, Mildred became militant in her campaign against him, seeking to enlist friends and acquaintances in an effort to get rid of him. Her talk became increasingly bitter, vindictive, and hostile. "If I had a gun, I'd kill that man!" she told an unsaved acquaintance.

What effect did Mildred's attitude have on herself and her family? Eventually she and her husband and three children dropped out of the church. And the last I heard of this family was that both parents were far from the Lord and their children had brought much grief to their hearts by their conduct.

This family did not have to come down to this sad place. For the Bible assures us:

> There hath no temptation taken you but such as is common to man: but God is faithful, who will not suffer you to be tempted above that ye are able; but will with the temptation also make a way to escape, that ye may be able to bear it (I Cor. 10:13).

When we are faced with situations that cause hostile or bitter thoughts to arise in our minds,

94

then we should flee to our Lord. Those thoughts are of the flesh and the devil. They are certainly not of God and, if entertained, will build a wall between us and God. Wrong thinking wrecks our peace of mind. If, for instance, Mildred considered that minister her enemy, then prayer for him would have been her most effective approach.

It may be that hostile, bitter thoughts arise because there is already sin in our hearts. Thus a sermon may convict us and make us angry. Or the godly, zealous life of another Christian can be a rebuke to our own; and so we might become jealous or resentful toward that person, and even build a case against him.

It's a terrible mistake, however, for us to allow these hostile thoughts to take over our minds, for they only increase unto more ungodliness. Rather we should go before the Lord and seek the cleansing power of His love for our hearts and minds.

What to do About Hostility

As long as we are in the flesh we are going to encounter trials of our patience. People will hurt, annoy, disappoint, or aggravate us. And we'll get angry, which will lead to hostile thoughts. If we entertain those hostile thoughts, the love we should have for others will disappear. The Holy Spirit will be grieved; and instead of His controlling our lives, the devil and sin will take over.

The best way to overcome hostility is to pray for those who despitefully use us, as Jesus said we should (Matt. 5:44). It's hard to be hostile toward someone for whom you're praying. And if you pray with love in your heart for that person, God might effect a necessary change in that person's life!

Another way is to learn to be more tolerant of the shortcomings of others. This shouldn't be hard to do if we continually remind ourselves how much God has forgiven us. Our daily prayer should be, "Forgive us our trespasses as we forgive those who trespass against us."

A command of Jesus could also be applied here— "Therefore all things whatsoever ye would that men should do to you, do ye even so to them ..." (Matt. 7:12). Do we want others to be patient, forgiving, and longsuffering toward us? Of course we do!

"Above all things have intense and unfailing love for one another," wrote Peter, "for love covers a multitude of sins—forgives and disregards the offenses of others" (I Pet. 4:8, *Amplified N.T.* See Prov. 10:12).

But how can we deal with sudden aggravations that come up? Well, the Bible says we should be slow to speak, slow to anger (Jas. 1:19, Prov. 16:32). How can we get into this habit? Many of us have developed the habit of speaking or acting first and then being sorry later—of losing our tempers.

Thomas Jefferson advised, "When angry count ten before you speak; if very angry, a hundred." That may be old advice, but it's still good. And, of course, awareness of God and instant prayer can save us from foolish temper.

Another way to avoid sinning when something angers us is to try to find something humorous in the whole thing. As Pediatrician I. Newton Kugelmass said in his book, *Growing Superior Children,* "When humor enters, anger departs."

Wholesome Outlets

What if we repress our rage, but it goes down into our subconscious and festers there? "The healthy course of emotional upheaval is to give it an outlet," says Dr. Abraham P. Sperling in *How to Make Psychology Work For You.* "Otherwise, it will be repressed and diverted into some unwholesome bit of compensatory behaviour."

The worst outlet, of course, is to fall in a rage on someone else; it's giving way to the sins of wrath and hatred, and perhaps even profanity. In many cases people don't unleash their rage against the one who caused it, but against a convenient scapegoat. A far better way and more acceptable in God's sight would be for us to work off those aggressive feelings into socially acceptable and even constructive channels.

God gave us these wonderful minds of ours—let's use them to ease the tensions that come to our bodies because of frustration, dismay, repressed anger, etc. Yes, we may fight down anger at times, but it may just lie there simmering. Let's use every means at our disposal to rid ourselves of harmful thoughts and feelings. Let's pray—and let's use physical means also.

We might try running or walking around the block, for instance. That'll not only reduce the steam, but be good for us physically. And on our little trip we'll see and hear some beautiful things that God has made, which will remind us of God's love. We might also engage in sports, or develop a hobby, or mow the lawn, or clean the house.

But above all we should talk to our Lord about the matter. For by bringing a problem to the surface and talking it out, we can let go of pent-up feelings that we shouldn't entertain. There is no better counselor to whom we can turn. The Bible says He is "the God of all comfort, Who comforteth us in all our tribulation" (II Cor. 1:4).

He heals the broken-hearted. He sets the prisoner of hate free. He opens the eyes of the blind, so that they can see the hostility in their hearts and replace it with His love. Yes, God is love, and He wants us to be love too.

"May the Lord direct your hearts into [realizing and showing] the love of God ..." (II Thess. 3:5, *Amplified N.T.*).

8

HUMILITY VERSUS PRIDE

"And whosoever shall exalt himself shall be abased; and he that shall humble himself shall be exalted."

(Matthew 23:12).

No doubt pride is the most sinful attitude of mind that man or angel could have. Christ condemned it even more than adultery. Pride led to the very first sin in the universe. When Satan's heart was lifted up, he proclaimed, "I will exalt my throne above the stars of God" (Isa. 14:13).

Pride led to the first sin of man, for it was his desire to exalt himself that made him disobey God. Pride caused God's chosen people, the Jews, to reject the Son of God, because they preferred to trust in their own works rather than God's provision (Rom. 9:31-32). Pride undoubtedly keeps more people out of Heaven than any other thing, because they will not humble themselves and become as little children (Matt. 18:3).

Alexander Pope wrote in his *Essay on Criticism:*

> Of all the causes which conspire to blind
> Man's erring judgment, and misguide the mind,
> What the weak head with strongest bias rules,
> Is pride—the never-failing vice of fools.

Pride causes people to be egotistic, self-righteous, self-assertive, derogatory, embittered, sarcastic, querulous, and resentful. A prideful person "builds mountains out of molehills." Although he readily offends others, he himself is very sensitive. He is often argumentative, uncompromising, and aggressive. When crossed he is likely to be sullen, morose, peevish, and irritable. He continually finds fault with others, and is chronically hostile and angry.

Interestingly enough, this is the description that Dr. Emanuel Messinger, senior psychiatrist at Bellevue Hospital in New York, gives of a paranoid personality in the Mental Health Encyclopedia found in most libraries today.

Dr. Messinger indicates that pride is the outstanding characteristic of paranoia. It may well be that the heart attitude of pride is what leads to the paranoid state of mind. In the Book of Proverbs such a person is called a fool, a scorner, and an ungodly man.

Speaking of a paranoid individual, Dr. Messinger says:

> He approaches others with a "chip on the shoulder" attitude. The drive for achievement may be intense and impel him to seek goals that are well beyond his capacity. Intolerant of criticism and unable to accept suggestions, he readily criticizes

100

and belittles others. Meticulous and precise, he is in some respects highly efficient, but because of his jealousy and inflexibility, he is prone to get into difficulties in situations where he needs to work harmoniously with others. He is driven to demonstrate his superiority and in a position of authority is very likely to become a petty tyrant.

Such a person creates a wretched home life for himself and his family because his pride with its resultant attitudes, makes him very difficult to get along with. Often when a man with this tendency in his personality makeup becomes a professing Christian, he does become a petty tyrant and worse in some respects than he was before. For he suddenly learns that according to the Bible he is the "head of the woman" and has the position of authority in the house. But the way in which he "snaps the whip" is not in accordance with the principles laid down in God's Word. For the man's rule over woman is not to be in tyranny, but in love.

Now most of us may not have such a great amount of pride as to be called paranoid, but we may certainly have enough of it to spoil our lives and testimonies for the Lord, to show itself in the various characteristics mentioned here.

The antidote for pride is humility. And the way to get humility is to humble ourselves. That's a definite act of our wills, our hearts, our minds!

It costs us our pride to humble ourselves. But it's the only sure way to true heart joy, and to peace and harmony in our lives. It's the only way to be right with God.

Pride—The Greatest Sin

One of the seven things that the Bible says God hates is "a proud look" (Prov. 6:16-17). Pride is called here an abomination to God. Proverbs 8:13 says, "The fear of the Lord is to hate evil: pride and arrogancy and the evil way and the forward mouth do I hate." And small wonder, for pride is the very antithesis of the fruit of God's Spirit (See Gal. 5:22-23).

Many Bible commentators agree that Ezekiel 28:12-18 is actually speaking of Satan. There it tells how beautiful, intelligent, and great he was. But God says, "Thine heart was lifted up because of thy beauty, thou has corrupted thy wisdom by reason of thy brightness: I will cast thee to the ground ..." His pride in himself caused him to pit his will against God's.

> The moment Lucifer, son of the morning, said "I will," that moment he became Satan, the father of the night. The shining one degenerated into the black devil of Scripture. No sooner was he a sinner than he was "satan," meaning the adversary of God. No sooner was he a traitor than he was "the devil," and accuser of God.—Ruth Paxson, *War in Your Heart*.

I submit that the original and greatest "paranoid personality" is Satan, and he infects those whose wills are not submitted to God's!

"All self-love gives Satan ground on which to

work," F.J. Huegel says. "Uncrucified flesh is gunpowder into which he will sooner or later throw a match, and a terrible conflagration may result."—*Forever Triumphant*.

Pride is the thing that causes men to think more highly of themselves than they should and to seek their own self-exaltation at the expense of others. This leads people to depend on their own self-righteousness for their salvation rather than on God. It leads them to be critical of others, to belittle them, and to belligerently defend their own ideas.

"Woe unto you, Pharisees!" said Jesus. "For ye love the uppermost seats in the synagogues and greetings in the markets. Woe unto you, scribes and Pharisees, hypocrites!" Yes, pride leads to great hypocrisy.

The Bible says:

> . . .God sets Himself against the proud and haughty, but gives grace [continually] to the lowly—those who are humble-minded. . . . Humble yourselves—feeling very insignificant—in the presence of the Lord, and He will exalt you (Jas. 4:6, 10, *Amplified N.T.*).

Pride and Contention

From whence comes the contention in our homes, communities, churches, and nations? From the pride of man. Jesus' disciples quarreled about who should be greatest. The Corinthian Christians argued about which group was the most important in the church. King Saul tried to kill David because the people were praising David more than him.

How many homes in this land are torn by dissension? It's hard to tell, because we can't see what goes on inside the homes. But many ministers know of the Hades on earth caused by the spirit of pride that rules one or both of the married partners.

The Bible says, "Only by pride cometh contention" (Prov. 13:10). Would you like a peaceful, Christ-honoring home? Then somebody has to humble himself!

"Man's basic characteristic is pride," says Norman B. Harrison. "Its one antidote is Christ's humility, ministered through the human channel of lives humbly yielded to Him. Our restlessness and discontent await this remedy."—*New Testament Living*.

The person who is full of pride lacks love, for the Bible says, "Love vaunteth not itself, is not puffed up" (I Cor. 13:4). Therefore such a person will not "walk in love" toward his fellow man. He'll always run into conflict with others. Hostility is pride's twin brother.

Thus the antidote for contention in churches is love coupled with humility. The Bible says, "Be kindly affectioned one to another with brotherly love; in honor preferring one another" (Rom. 12:10).

And the Philippians were told, "Let nothing be done through strife or vain glory; but in lowliness of mind let each esteem other better than themselves" (Phil. 2:3).

Since a scorner will not hear rebuke (Prov. 13:1), perhaps the only answer to achieving peace can be found in Proverbs 22:10—"Cast out the scorner and contention shall go out; yea, strife and reproach shall cease." (See I Tim. 6:3-5.) Some people are so full of pride they may never change.

Pride and Contention

God often humbles men, however. He does it by chastisement. A good example of this is what happened to King Nebuchadnezzar. "Is not this great Babylon, that I have built ... by the might of my power, and for the honor of my majesty?" he boasted. Within an hour King Nebuchadnezzar became like an animal—his hair like eagles' feathers and his nails like birds' claws—and he was driven from men and "did eat grass as oxen" (Dan. 4:33).

At the end of seven years Nebuchadnezzar lifted up his eyes unto heaven. His understanding returned—and he gave honor to God, instead of himself.

Yes, people often bring much trouble and heartache on themselves because of their pride, their unwillingness to yield their wills to God's. "Pride goeth before destruction, and an haughty spirit before a fall," says Proverbs 16:18.

A stubborn mule must be beaten and a wild horse hobbled. But greatly blessed is the one who humbles himself. "The meek will he *guide* in judgment, and the meek will he *teach* his way" (Psa. 25:9).

Pride and Vanity

Satan was the first one whose heart was lifted up by vanity. And then after that I guess came women! Satan knew what he was doing when he went to Eve first—and he appealed to her vanity. Also, it was the women of Israel the Lord rebuked on this fault by way of Isaiah:

> Moreover the Lord saith, Because the daughters of Zion are haughty and walk with stretched forth necks and wanton eyes, walking and mincing as they go, and making a tinkling with their feet: therefore the Lord will smite ... (Isa. 3:16-17a).

The Apostle Peter cautioned Christian women not to depend so much on their outward appearance to win their husbands to the Lord as on their inward spirit of humility (I Pet. 3:1-6). He is not advising here that a woman become a plain-looking, unattractive character who causes her husband to become repelled by what he thinks is Christianity. Rather he is advising that she attach more importance to a sweetness of spirit than to anything that might increase her vanity and self-centeredness.

Many men also have a tendency to be vain and can be led astray by women who appeal to their vanity with admiration. We need to remember that the more vain we become about our appearance or accomplishments, the more like the devil we become, and the less like Christ.

Pride and Wrath

The Hebrew word for pride also can be translated "raging." Thus it can be said that the person easily given to anger and wrath is a person full of pride. "Proud and haughty scorner is his name, who dealeth in proud wrath," says Proverbs 21:24.

> For wrath is the daughter of pride.... A person truly humbled permits not anything to put him in a rage. As it is pride which dies last in the soul, so it is passion which is last destroyed in the outward conduct. A soul thoroughly dead to itself, finds nothing of rage left.—Madame Guyon.

I have a dear friend who had a terrible temper before she received Christ as her Saviour. She even at times threatened her husband with a butcher knife. But after she yielded her heart to Christ, she became a wonderful example of Christian love to him, so that he too came to the Saviour.

Humility—The Mind of Christ

"Let this mind be in you, which was also in Christ Jesus" (Phil. 2:5). Whenever I read the second chapter of Philippians I stand in awe at the humility of our Lord Jesus Christ. Just think, He Who was Creator of all things humbled Himself beyond all of our imagination. The God of the universe took on the body of a man. And as if that weren't enough, He died for us on the cross and took our loathsome sins on Himself too, so that we might be saved.

Jesus was born in the most humble circumstances, so that even the most lowly person could identify himself with the Son of man. He would not even allow the Jews to crown Him as king, because He cared more for men's eternal condition than He did for their momentary elevation.

"Take my yoke upon you and learn of me," said Jesus, "for I am meek and lowly in heart; and ye shall find rest unto your souls" (Matt. 11:29). Do you seek the secret of happiness and peace? There it is, in yielding to God and becoming meek and lowly in heart! Andrew Murray once said:

> When I look back upon my own religious experience or upon the church of Christ in the world, I stand amazed at the thought of how little humility is sought after as the distinguishing feature of the discipleship of Jesus. In preaching and living, in the daily intercourse of the home and social life, in the more special fellowship with Christians, in the direction and performance of work for Christ—how much proof there is that humility is not esteemed the cardinal virtue, the root from which the graces grow, the one indispensable condition of true fellowship with Jesus.

"Let this mind be in you," the Bible says, and here again we see the power of right thinking. For having Christ's mind and thinking humbly of one's self instead of proudly is one of the great secrets of a happy, useful life.

108

"How shall we become Christlike?" Dr. Norman B. Harrison propounds in *New Testament Living*. "Not by imitating His life's outwardness but by laying hold of its inwardness—its inner mindedness. . . . Christ's life was the expression of His mind: an unselfed mind, giving up all His glory; a humbleness of mind, more lowly than His fellows; a mind to suffer, even to the Cross."

One need not think ill of himself to be humble. One need not have what psychiatrists call "a poor self-image." Jesus didn't. Jesus said, "Love thy neighbor as thyself."

If we are beloved of God and His children through faith in Christ, then we are not only heirs of the Kingdom of God, but potential heirs of His gracious qualities as well. These blessed spiritual qualities can be had, however, only on the condition that we humble ourselves and allow Christ to live in and through us. Andrew Murray wrote:

> The blessedness of a Christlike humility is unspeakable. It is of great worth in the sight of God. "He giveth grace to the humble." In the spiritual life it is the source of rest and joy. To the humble all God does is right and good. Humility is always ready to praise God for the least of His mercies. Humility does not find it difficult to trust. It submits unconditionally to all that God says.—*Like Christ*.

"Someone asked Augustine what was the first of the religious graces," D.L. Moody wrote in *The Overcoming Life*, "and he said, 'Humility.' They asked him what was the second, and he replied,

'Humility.' They asked him the third, and he said, 'Humility.' I think that if we are humble, we have all the graces."

The more we see God in His infinite, matchless, perfect love and grace, the more humble we must become. This is why you can usually tell which Christians are in the habit of spending time with the Lord each day in communion and Bible reading—and which ones are not. For as we think about Him, we cannot help but fall in wonder at His feet.

When the great prophet Isaiah saw the Lord, he cried, "Woe is me! For I am undone; because I am a man of unclean lips, and I dwell in the midst of a people of unclean lips; for mine eyes have seen the King, the Lord of hosts" (Isa. 6:5). Jeremiah and Moses had similar feelings of unworthiness and humility when they saw the Lord (Jer. 1:6; Ex. 3:11).

"Put on ... humbleness of mind," the Apostle Paul wrote the Colossians by the Spirit (Col. 3:12). Therefore, casting aside our pride and becoming humble is a definite act of our wills—in response to a command from God.

The Amplified Version of the New Testament gives us an expanded view of the Apostle Peter's message from God on this subject:

> Clothe ... yourselves, all of you, with humility— as the garb of a servant, so that its covering cannot possibly be stripped from you, with freedom from pride and arrogance—toward one another. For God sets Himself against the proud—the insolent, the over-bearing, the disdainful, the presumptuous, the boastful, and opposes, frustrates

and defeats them—but gives grace (favor, blessing) to the humble.... Therefore humble yourselves (demote, lower yourselves in your own estimation) under the mighty hand of God, that in due time He may exalt you (I Pet. 5:5-6).

9
OTHER ATTITUDES OF MIND

Create in me a clean heart, O God; and renew a right spirit within me.
—Psalm 51:10.

What is your general way of thinking? Is it negative or positive? Many secular and religious books deal with this subject from the human standpoint and the advice they give often can be helpful. Sometimes people do overcome negative hang-ups by sheer power of will. In other cases, they may seek God's help and get it.

Drs. Barry and Patricia Bricklin, psychologists on the faculty of Hahnemann Medical College in Philadelphia, write, "Our experience has convinced us there is a large body of people who ensnare themselves in chronic neurotic interactions that are fed by the exchange of intensely negative emotions. These interactions are doomed to endless repetition unless the negative emotions are reduced."—*Strong Family, Strong Child.*

What are negative emotions? Hate, anger, fear— these are some of the basic ones. These in turn give rise to negative frames of mind. Instead of loving, we hate—or we smoulder with hostility. Instead of trusting, we fear. Instead of caring about others, we are self-centered and therefore full of self-defensive pride. Instead of yielding to God, we are afraid that it will cost us something—so we stubbornly go the other way.

"Bitterness and hatred, sorrow and grief, worry and care, anxiety and fear, may be concealed in the heart until it overflows with the burden, and "Out of the abundance of the heart the mouth speaketh," says Dr. L. Gilbert Little in *Nervous Christians*.

We have already dealt with some of these negative attitudes as compared to their opposites. But there are a number of other negative attitudes that people allow to dominate their thinking that not only make them miserable people, but also destroy their Christian testimonies. We will touch on some of these in this chapter, along with their positive opposites.

Thankfulness, Praise, and Cheerfulness versus Complaining

Complaining on the part of His people always grieves the heart of God. It indicates that they are not satisfied with His will in their lives, that they don't believe that He knows best. It shows a lack of faith. Praying about something is one thing— complaining is another!

A number of times the Children of Israel complained against God and His chosen leader Moses

113

when they were wandering in the wilderness. And several times the Lord brought judgment on them for their complaining and lack of faith.

"And do not grumble, as some of them did," said the Apostle Paul to the Corinthians, "and they were destroyed by the Destroyer. All this happened to them by way of warning; but it was recorded by way of admonition to us who live in the last days of the world" (I Cor. 10:10-11, *Weymouth N.T.*).

Complainers are miserable people and they make others miserable too. In addition, there is nothing so catching as a complaining spirit! It spread like wildfire among the Israelites. And it spreads like wildfire in churches today.

> Ungrateful Christians receive no new blessings. Although the Lord is a generous and willing giver, the measure of our actually being blessed is dependent upon our practical gratefulness and devotion. How foolish therefore to lament and groan instead of rejoicing in God's goodness. By worrying we are robbing ourselves. Unthankfulness leads to spiritual poverty. But our whole life should be a constant practical thank-offering full of joy.—Erich Sauer, *In the Arena of Faith.*

There is nothing like praising God daily to create a thankful spirit in us. For when we praise God we can't help but think of all that He has done for us. Our salvation alone should fill our hearts with eternal gratitude. What a tremendous blessing and privilege it is to know God personally and to have His help and comfort constantly available! What a blessing not to fear death!

114

We should be like the Psalmist who said by God's inspiration:

> I will bless the Lord at all times: his praise shall continually be in my mouth. My soul shall make her boast in the Lord; the humble shall hear thereof, and be glad. O magnify the Lord with me, and let us exalt his name together. I sought the Lord and he heard me, and delivered me from all my fears (Psa. 34:1-4).

A thankful spirit will make you a cheerful person, a person whom other people enjoy being with. Who enjoys listening to a complainer? No one, really. On the other hand, what a pleasure it is to have fellowship with a cheerful, thankful person who radiates his love for Christ!

According to God's Word, such a person should not only enjoy good health himself, but his presence and words will help others to have good health too. The Bible says, "Pleasant words are as a honeycomb, sweet to the mind and healing to the body" (Prov. 16:24, *Amplified Old Testament*, Zondervan, 1962).

Conversely, a complaining, critical, pessimistic person would tend to have poorer health and afflict his family with the same. Proverbs 17:22 says, "A happy heart is a good medicine and a cheerful mind works healing, but a broken spirit dries the bones" (*Amplified Old Testament*, Zondervan, 1962). The Lord is able to heal the broken spirit and pessimistic mind. Yes, He can cheer us up if we'll let Him!

The cheerful, thankful person has an inward

beauty that is radiated in his pleasant countenance. It makes him appear beautiful to others. In a newspaper I read the following:

> A ready smile, an instinct to speak well of others and to be sympathetic to them, a serenity in the face of one's own problems—these are the things of inner beauty. As with all beauty treatments, they must be practiced conscientiously and consistently. Think beauty until it becomes second nature.

The Holy Spirit is the One Who can impart to us a beautiful nature.

For if we have the joy of the Holy Spirit in our hearts, we can have the frame of mind that the Apostles had. Paul, who encountered great suffering all through his Christian life, had a beautiful nature. He wrote to the Philippians, "Rejoice in the Lord always: and again I say, Rejoice." Later he added, "I have learned, in whatsoever state I am, therewith to be content" (Phil. 4:4, 11).

To the Corinthians Paul wrote, "I am filled with comfort, I am exceeding joyful in all our tribulation" (II Cor. 7:4). Paul's joy was not as the world giveth, but that which Christ Jesus promised!

James wrote, "You must consider it the purest joy, my brothers, when you are involved in various trials, for you surely know that what is genuine in your faith produces the patient mind that endures" (Jas. 1:2-3, *Williams N.T.*).

And Peter wrote, "But rejoice, inasmuch as ye are partakers of Christ's sufferings; that, when His glory shall be revealed, ye may be glad also with exceeding joy" (I Pet. 4:13). He also wrote, "Whom having not seen, ye love; in whom, though now ye see Him not, yet believing, ye rejoice with joy unspeakable and full of glory" (I Pet. 1:8).

The Bible confirms that such a heart attitude depends on being filled with the Holy Spirit. The Apostle Paul wrote:

> . . .Be filled with the Spirit; speaking to yourselves in psalms and hymns and spiritual songs, singing and making melody in your heart to the Lord; giving thanks always for all things unto God and the Father in the name of our Lord Jesus Christ (Eph. 5:18-20).

"Therefore away with all grumbling!" exclaims Eric Sauer. "All spirit of complaint and dissatisfaction is rebellion against God. God is always right. 'Love your destiny, for it is God's way with your soul.' "—*In the Arena of Faith*.

Forgiving versus Holding Grudges

No doubt one of the most soul-destroying practices is that of holding grudges in our hearts, allowing bitterness, anger, and hostility to fester there. These eat right down into our subconscious like a cancer and permeate our whole personalities.

No wonder our Lord said, "And when ye stand praying, forgive, if ye have ought against any, that your Father also which is in heaven may forgive you your trespasses. But if ye do not forgive, neither will your Father which is heaven forgive your trespasses" (Mark 11:25-26).

Jesus went even further than that, however, in his prescription for righteous and joyful living, when He said, "But I say unto you, Love your enemies, bless them that curse you, do good to them that hate you, and pray for them which despitefully use you and persecute you" (Matt. 5:44). This of course can only be done by the power of the Holy Spirit.

Many people, even Christians, have mental and emotional hang-ups that spoil their lives and happiness. The reason for this in some cases may lie deep in their subconscious, according to psychologists. I'll go along with this. Perhaps deep in their hearts they have never forgiven their parents or themselves for something. And so deep inside they have either hostility and bitterness toward their parents or hatred for themselves.

I believe the Holy Spirit is able to show us if we have these deep-seated feelings and He is able to root them out—if we will yield completely to Him. The Lord Jesus promised, "But when the Spirit of truth comes, He will guide you into the whole truth" (John 16:13, *Williams*).

Almost always the spirit of unforgiveness goes hand in hand with bitterness and resentment, which in turn keeps the Holy Spirit from filling our hearts with His power and love. In his book, *Release From Tension*, Dr. Paul E. Adolph says:

> The Word of God makes it clear that it is bitterness and resentment that bar the way to forgive-

ness, for it is clearly pointed out that the grace of God is the antithesis of bitterness in Hebrews 12:15 where we are admonished to be "looking diligently lest any man fail of the grace of God." This failure on one's part to appropriate the grace of God is further attributed in this Scripture to "any root of bitterness springing up" so as to trouble us and defile many. It is clear that the spirit of bitterness and resentment and the fullness of God's grace cannot coexist in the same human heart.

If one truly forgives, he will put out of his heart-mind all thoughts of bitterness and resentment that he may have had toward the person he forgives. He will keep them out too. This clears the way for the love of God to fill the heart and overflow to all others with whom he comes into contact.

Giving versus Taking

This may sound more like something we may do rather than something we may think—but actually, don't these ways of living spring from our attitudes of mind? Isn't it the basically selfish person who is always the recipient of thoughtful kindnesses on the part of others, and never the giver of unsolicited help—unless it be for the purpose of self-glorification?

Such a person *thinks* of himself first—always. The giving type of person, on the other hand, has his thoughts filled with others. *How can I help them? How can I comfort? What can I do to ease the burden?*

A born-again child of God should always be a giver. Not that it's wrong to partake of the kindness and help of others—oh, no! We should do that gratefully, for the Lord wants us to help each other; and when we need help, we should accept it graciously from God's messengers of mercy. But I mean, in our hearts we should be givers. And if we have that heart attitude, then God can use us—our time, our talent, our energy, our money—to answer the prayers of others who need what we have to give.

The Lord Jesus said, "It is more blessed to give than to receive" (Acts 20:35).

Success in business or career also frequently depends on being a giver. Henry Ford said:

> Success is not rare—it is common. Very few miss a measure of it. It is not a matter of luck or contesting, for certainly, no success can come from preventing the success of another. It is a matter of adjusting one's efforts to obstacles and one's abilities to a service needed by others. There is no other possible success. But most people think of it in terms of getting; success, however, begins in terms of giving.

The happiest people I know are givers. Genie, a friend of mine in South Carolina, works full-time to support herself; she gives all of her spare time for the betterment of the lives of black young people. She plans Christian rallies for them, encourages them personally to live for Christ, and each summer makes it possible for between 100 and 150 black teenagers to attend a Christian Bible camp. This has inspired a number of these fellows and girls to dedicate their lives to Christ.

If we truly are thankful to God for all the blessings He has bestowed on us, then we will consider that everything we have belongs to Him and should be at His disposal. Besides giving time, talent, and energy to doing His will, we will want to support His work in all parts of the world, as well as in our own church and community.

I've heard it said, "We can't outgive God." And we can't. If we don't give with the idea of getting, He oftens showers us with material blessings (Mal. 3:10). I've seen this proved in my own life. The Bible says:

> But this I say, He which soweth sparingly shall reap also sparingly; and he which soweth bountifully shall reap also bountifully. Every man according as he *purposeth* in his *heart,* so let him give; not grudgingly, or of necessity: for God loveth a cheerful giver.

Judging Others versus Facing Self

The person who is constantly criticizing and finding fault with others is a very unhappy person. He may be what the psychologists call either "neurotic" or "paranoid." He is usually trying to build up his own ego at the expense of others. And he is violating a teaching of the Son of God by doing so. The Lord Jesus said:

> Judge not, that ye be not judged. For with what judgment ye judge, ye shall be judged: and with what measure ye mete, it shall be measured to you again. And why beholdest thou the mote that is in thy brother's eye, but considerest not the beam that is in thine own eye? .... Thou hypocrite, first cast out the beam out of thine own eye; and then shall thou see clearly to cast out the mote out of thy brother's eye.—Matthew 7:1-5.

A friend of mine in New Jersey had been having a turbulent life with her husband. She thought he was to blame. Not long after she became a Christian, however, her pastor preached on the above text. My friend decided to put it into practice in relation to her husband and herself.

She examined her own actions, to see what she had been doing to add to the conflict. To her surpise she saw that there were a number of ways in which she had contributed to it. "Lord, help me to be more cooperative and understanding," she prayed. With prayer, watchfulness, and God's help, she was able to bring a much more peaceful atmosphere to her home.

In *The Calvary Road* Roy Hession writes:

> I suggest that the beam in our eye is simply our unloving reaction to the other man's mote. Without doubt there is a wrong in the other person. But our reaction to that wrong is wrong too! The mote in him has provoked us to resentment, or coldness, or criticism, or bitterness, or evil speaking, or ill will—all of them variants of the basic ill, unlove. And that, says the Lord Jesus, is far, far worse than the tiny wrong (sometimes quite unconscious) that provoked it.

Dr. L. Gilbert Little believes that the devil encourages people in critical or condemnatory thinking. "Another of Satan's tricks today is to cause God's people to have evil thoughts about others. A common method is to get us to attribute wrong motives to their actions. This, too, is giving way to vain imaginations."—*Nervous Christians*.

Judging others begins in the heart-mind. We brood over real or imagined wrongs. We attribute to others false motives. We deliberately look for faults in others perhaps to excuse our own shortcomings. The prime remedy for this, as Jesus said, is for us to quit looking at others and examine ourselves.

"But why dost thou judge thy brother?" asked the Apostle Paul. "Or why dost thou set at nought thy brother? For we shall all stand before the judgment seat of Christ. . . . Every one of us shall give account of himself to God" (Rom. 14:10-12).

We harm ourselves—our hearts, our minds—when it is our practice to judge our brothers. But we save ourselves a great deal of heartache and unhappiness if we examine and judge ourselves. The Bible says, "For if we would judge ourselves, we should not be judged. But when we are judged, we are chastened of the Lord, that we should not be condemned with the world" (I Cor. 11:31-32).

There are some instances wherein Christians must judge or take a stand. But care needs to be taken that such judgment or stand is in accordance with Biblical teachings. What we're discussing here are individual judgments that we may make because of a basic lack of love in our hearts toward others.

"Sometimes when a person would find his true thoughts and feelings intolerable," says psychologist Floyd L. Ruch in his book, *Psychology and Life*, "he not only represses them but also convinces himself unconsciously that other people have these thoughts and feelings toward him. By this mechanism of projection the individual is able to direct his aggressive feelings toward others rather than toward himself.

"Projection also enables a person to blame other people—or even things—for failures that are essentially of his own making."

How can we who are Christians avoid using this neurotic device that hinders our Christian life? By setting our hearts on God instead of ourselves. In his *Institutes of the Christian Religion* John Calvin wrote:

> It is plain that no man can arrive at the true knowledge of himself, without having first contemplated the divine character, and then descended to the consideration of his own. For, such is the native pride of us all, we invariably esteem ourselves righteous, innocent, wise, and holy, till we are convinced, by clear proofs, of our unrighteousness, turpitude, folly, and impurity. But we are never thus convinced, while we confine our attention to ourselves, and regard not the Lord, who is the only standard by which this judgment ought to be formed. Because, from our natural proneness to hypocrisy, any vain appearance of righteousness abundantly contents us instead of the reality.

As we meditate on the goodness, faithfulness, righteousness, and love of God, we can't help but be convicted of how far short we fall! This humbles us and prepares us to listen to the counsel of others, even as my New Jersey friend did. Roy Hession says, "There are blind spots in all our lives that we shall never see, unless we are prepared for another to be God's channel to us."—*The Calvary Road*.

In his book, *The Struggle For Peace*, Dr. Henry R. Brandt tells about an unhappy professing Christian named George who sought help at a mental clinic. After the counselor probed for a while, George finally blew his top. And the counselor then pointed out that George was really filled with anger and hatred toward people, not love, as he had thought.

The man finally consulted Dr. Brandt. "Since this counselor forced me to blow up," he related, "I've been pretty nasty to a lot of people." What evil thing, he wanted to know, had the counselor done to him? Dr. Brandt told him that the counselor had forced him to face the truth about himself.

"Man is miserable when he does not take responsibility for his own inner life, his own reactions and behaviour toward the people and circumstances that come his way," says Dr. Brandt.

The power of right thinking in this area, therefore, lies in honestly facing ourselves, considering our own shortcomings, and seeking God's power to overcome. If we want others to have tolerance and patience toward us, then we must have the tolerance and patience toward them that our loving, holy God has toward us!

"So, since we have such promises as these, dearly beloved, let us cleanse ourselves from everything that defiles our bodies and spirits, and in reverence to God carry on our consecration to completeness" (II Cor. 7:1, Williams N.T.).

10
HEART COMMUNICATIONS WITH GOD

> So if you have been raised to life in fellowship with Christ, keep on seeking the things above, where Christ is seated at the right hand of God. Practice occupying your minds with the things above, not with the things on earth; for you have died, and your life is now hidden in God through your fellowship with Christ. When Christ, who is our life, appears, you too will appear to be glorified in fellowship with Him.—Colossians 3:1-4, Williams New Testament.

Communication is one mind touching another in some way. Now there are many people who pray to God, people in all kinds of religions, of all kinds of beliefs. Some say rote prayers, some say their prayers to be heard of men, some never think to pray except when they're in trouble. But are they really communicating with God?

According to Dr. H.A. Ironside, "It is wrong and foolish to try to set bounds to the mercy of God. He who hears the prayer of the young ravens when they cry for food, hears the agonized heart-cries of troubled men who are of 'more value than many sparrows' in His eyes. Both Scripture and history testify to prayers answered in wondrous grace, even when those who prayed were ignorant of the One to whom their entreaties were directed."—*Praying in the Holy Spirit.*

Thus God, being omniscient in all things, can certainly hear and help His creatures. But the hardness, sin, and unbelief in men's hearts often make the heavens "like brass" as far as they are concerned. The Bible says:

> Behold, the Lord's hand is not shortened, that it cannot save; neither his ear heavy, that it cannot hear: But your iniquities have separated between you and your God, and your sins have hid his face from you, that he will not hear (Isa. 59:1-2).

That is why Jesus Christ, God's son, said, "I am the way, the truth, and the life; no man cometh unto the Father but by me" (John 14:6). Through His death and shed blood on the cross, He made it possible for our sins to be taken away, forgiven by God. He made it possible for us to have new hearts.

Christ Jesus, the God-man, reconciled man with God (Rom. 5:10). He made daily communication with God possible for every person who receives Him as his Saviour. And He sealed the promise by sending His Spirit into the heart of every person who truly believes (II Cor. 1:22).

The Bible says, "If we confess our sins, He is faithful and just to forgive us our sins and to

128

cleanse us from all unrighteousness" (I John 1:9). The Apostle John actually wrote this to people who were already believers in Christ. For believers also have a tendency to allow sin to mar their communication with God.

This is why many take so little delight in spending time with their Lord each day! They're not on praying ground. They prefer to be busy, busy, busy—rather than to take the chance of hearing God speak to their hearts in the quietness of their room.

The Bible says, "If I regard iniquity in my heart, the Lord will not hear me" (Psa. 66:18). No wonder so few Christians can testify to recent answered prayer! They have a form of godliness, but not the power.

Observe in this scripture also how the thoughts of the mind are linked with the heart. We may be considered good Christians by others, but God knows where we stand in our hearts. And He wants us to get right with Him and put those wicked thoughts out! How can we be filled with His Spirit until we do? How can we expect prayers to be answered?

The Spiritual Battle

What can we do if because of our sinfulness and coldness of heart we have no desire to read God's Word or pray? I think then we should force ourselves to do it. For the Bible says, "Wherewithal shall a young man cleanse his way? By taking heed thereto according to thy word" (Psa. 119:9).

The Holy Spirit convicts and speaks to our hearts by God's Word. The Bible says:

> For the Word of God is quick and powerful, and sharper than any two-edged sword, piercing even to the dividing asunder of soul and spirit, and of the joints and marrow, and is a discerner of the thoughts and intents of the heart" (Heb. 4:12).

One side of us—the old Adamic nature—is going to fight tooth and nail against our reading God's Word because that part of us hates to give up control. Speaking of the carnal man or the back-slider in heart, Spurgeon wrote:

> The first kind of fulness with his own ways is absorption in his carnal pursuits. He has not much time to spend upon religion; he has other things to attend to. If you speak to him of the deep things of God, he is weary of you and even of the daily necessaries of godliness he has no care to hear much, except at service time. He has his business to see to, or he has to go out to a dinner party, or a few friends are coming to spend the evening: in any case, his answer to you is "I pray thee have me excused." Now, this pre-occupation with trifles is always mischievous, for when the soul is filled with chaff, there is no room left for wheat; when all your mind is taken up with frivolities, the weighty matters of eternity cannot enter.—*The Treasury of Charles H. Spurgeon.*

If we do become convicted of our occupation with worldly matters and sit down to read God's

Word, there's another enemy, Satan, who works hard to either snatch it away or get us to apply its admonitions to someone else. That's the old projection device. Or he has all kinds of other rationalizations handy for us to apply. This explains why some people can read the Word of God, as well as good books on victory, and it never seems to make a difference in their lives.

Therefore, when we read God's Word, we need to come to it honestly, and humbly ask God, "Open my eyes that I may see."

According to God's Word we're in a spiritual warfare, with mighty powers of darkness arrayed against us (Eph. 6:11-12). We dare not ignore this fact! If we do, we're in great danger from these forces. The Bible says we must put on God's whole armor—truth, righteousness, the preparation of the gospel of peace, faith, salvation, and the Word of God (Eph. 6:13-17). Added to this, Paul stresses the necessity of "praying always with all prayer and supplication in the spirit" (Eph. 6:18).

If we don't obey this advice, then we're leaving our minds and bodies open to attack from forces that are stronger than we are. But the Bible says, "Greater is he that is in you than he that is in the world" (I John 4:4). If we walk with the Lord, we need not fear the enemy.

Studying God's Word

The Bible says, "Study to shew thyself approved unto God, a workman that needeth not to be ashamed, rightly dividing the word of truth" (II Tim. 2:15).

"The highest secret of Bible study," wrote Arthur T. Pierson, "is that teachable spirit which is inseparable from obedience.... Our Lord says, 'If any man will do His will he shall know of the doctrine' (John 7:17); in other words, obedience is the organ of spiritual revelation."—*Knowing the Scriptures*.

Reading the Bible develops a hunger to read the Bible, as its cleansing effect begins to work on our hearts. The process works in a cycle: the more we read, the more we want to read; the less we read, the less we want to read.

James M. Gray wrote, "In this Word of God are given to us 'exceeding great and precious promises,' and as we come to know and desire them the process has a cleansing and separating effect upon our lives."—*Salvation From Start to Finish*.

The Apostle Peter confirms that before a person can have a normal healthy appetite for God's Word, he must cleanse out of his heart and life certain bad attitudes or ways of thinking. These include "every trace of wickedness (depravity, malignity) and all deceit and insincerity (pretence, hypocrisy) and grudges (envy, jealousy) and slander and evil speaking of every kind" (I Pet. 2:1, *Amplified N.T.*).

Then Peter says, "As newborn babes, desire the sincere milk of the word, that ye may grow thereby" (I Pet. 2:2). One of the first indications that a person has been truly born again by God's Spirit is his hunger for God's Word, for it is food for his new spirit.

He literally devours it; his hungry heart yearns for it. That's because his sins have just been forgiven; and he's a bright, shiny new Christian, eager to please the Lord in every way. Well, Peter says we should keep on being that way!

A daily cleansing by the washing of the water of God's Word, a daily admission of our shortcomings and unworthiness, a daily turning from sinful thoughts and attitudes—these keep us shiny bright Christians! And these can restore us to that joyful state. The Bible says, "The backslider gets bored with himself; the godly man's life is exciting" (Prov. 14:14, *Living Psalms and Proverbs*).

Joy and peace are a part of our inheritance as Christians. Why on earth do we drag along wearily through this world without them? Why do we take on the battles of life alone when we have an all-powerful Father Who will help us if we'll only obey Him?

The Bible is full of God's advice on how we can get the most out of life. Proverbs 6:23 says, "For the commandment is a lamp, and the law is light; and reproofs of instruction are the way of life."

Along a similar vein Psalm 119:105 says, "Thy word is a lamp unto my feet and a light unto my path." Why should we stumble blindly along life's path, falling into quagmires and traps that bring us grief, when it isn't necessary? But the key to our being guided past the pitfalls is obedience.

"The student of the Bible who would get the greatest profit out of his studies must be obedient to its teachings as soon as he sees them," wrote R.A. Torrey. "It was good advice James gave to early Christians, and to us, 'Be ye doers of the word and not hearers only, deceiving your own selves.' "—*The Treasury of R.A. Torrey*.

There is nothing so sweet as to have the Spirit open our eyes to the truths contained in God's Word. Sometimes I have mulled and prayed over a certain scripture, seeking the true meaning of it. And like a burst of lightning the meaning has struck me at times, thrilling me to my very soul. "Why have I never seen this before?" I have wondered.

After I had my second child, the Lord enlightened my understanding of John 3:5, which had often puzzled me. "Jesus answered, Verily, verily, I say unto thee, Except a man be born of water and of the Spirit, he cannot enter into the kingdom of God." Why, of course! The first time we are born, of the flesh, it is by water—for the water sac surrounding and protecting the baby first breaks open to facilitate the birth of the child. And our second birth must be by God's Spirit.

Sometimes revelation comes by reading surrounding verses. Sometimes it comes by looking up other references. Sometimes the writings of other saints of God can help us. And sometimes enlightenment comes merely by reading the verse over and over again. But always it comes by revelation of the blessed Holy Spirit of God.

Prayer

One of the best ways to get into a prayerful mood is to read several psalms. The psalms reveal a thankful heart. They contain testimonies of answered prayer and precious promises. They show repentance of sin. They give comfort and impart faith.

When we go to the Lord in prayer, we must always go in faith. "Without faith it is impossible to please him" says Hebrews 11:6. We must believe that our God is a prayer-hearing, prayer-answering God. And as we see prayers answered, we'll have more answered, because our faith is increased!

Some years ago I served as pianist at a small church in Plainfield, N.J., while the pastor and his wife visited their homeland in Europe for the summer. The man in charge of the prayer meeting made a big chart showing prayer requests. When our prayers were answered, he noted the answer on the chart. Since then I too have made my own list—and what a thrill it is to mark down the answers to prayers in red ink!

This way of praying demands that we make our prayers specific. Let us name names, mention details, bring every problem big and small to our Father in Heaven.

One prayer I prayed down to the last detail was

about the need of getting a job. (My husband was going to Bible college at the time.) I asked the Lord for a job within walking distance of my home; for a job where the hours would coincide closely with my daughter's school hours; for a good-paying job with lots of benefits; for a job I would enjoy; and for several other small particulars too.

The Lord gave me a position within one week that met every request! When we are in His will, He delights in giving us a cup running over! Some Christians feel we should never ask God for anything for ourselves. But why not? He's our Father, isn't He?

Jesus said, "If ye have faith as a grain of mustard seed, ye shall say unto this mountain, Remove hence to yonder place; and it shall remove; and nothing shall be impossible unto you" (Matt. 17:20). After I came to the Lord, I asked Him to save every member of my family—and one by one He did. Of course I backed my faith up with witnessing and working toward that goal. How can we expect the Lord to answer our prayers if we don't do what we're supposed to do?

What kind of Christianity do we have if we cannot testify to having our prayers answered? As Dr. John R. Rice says, "If Christianity is the true religion, and if God be a miracle-working, prayer-hearing, prayer-answering God, then the unsaved world has a right to demand that we prove it by having our prayers answered. . . . How doubts would flee away if we should begin to pray boldly and definitely and expect God to give concrete and specific answers to our prayers day by day!"—*Prayer—Asking and Receiving*.

There's a little gospel song entitled "Faith is Just Believing"—and so it is! Here again we see the power of right thinking exhibited, in prayer and the answer to prayer. Are we expecting our prayers to be answered? Or do we ritually throw up general prayers daily and miss out on one of the greatest privileges accorded to Christians by God?

The Bible says that when someone asks God for wisdom, he must ask in faith, without doubting. The person who doubts will not get anything he asks for. "[For being as he is] a man of *two minds*—hesitating, dubious, irresolute—[he is] unstable and unreliable and uncertain about everything he thinks (feels, decides)" (Jas. 1:8, *Amplified N.T.*).

We also must pray with a consciousness of the presence of the Holy Spirit, for He is our co-partner in prayer. "Likewise the Spirit also helpeth our infirmities: for we know not what we should pray for as we ought: but the Spirit itself maketh intercession for us with groanings which cannot be uttered" (Rom. 8:26). Praying in the Spirit depends on our submission to God and realization of our utter dependence upon Him.

"I tell you, you might be on your knees till your knees were bare," wrote Spurgeon, "and you might be in your closet till the steam of your devotion ran down the walls, but unless the Spirit of the Lord was in that closet with you, the mere fleshly exercise of praying would no more avail you and profit you than if you had been chanting songs to the moon or standing in the street to sell your goods."—*The Treasury of Charles H. Spurgeon.*

As Robert Cook says, "The secret of unanswered prayer is incomplete surrender (Jas. 4:3)."—*Now That I believe.*

It isn't always easy to pray. The natural man in us can think of a dozen other things we must be doing! It takes self-discipline to pray. It takes the conviction that prayer works—that God can do more than all of our human efforts put together (although in many cases He uses us as His instruments to accomplish His will). Sometimes it takes persistence—a constant rapping on the door of Heaven (Luke 11:5-8; 18:1-7). Many women have seen their husbands come to Christ through this kind of prayer.

Leonard Ravenhill writes, "Prayer is taxing. Prayer is exacting. Prayer means enduring. Prayer means denying self, a daily dying by choice."—*Revival Praying.* Yes, prayer costs something—but the blessings it brings into our lives far surpass the cost! Answered prayer gives us joy and thanksgiving in our hearts, it fills our minds with faith and confidence in our God, and it floods our souls with the peace that passeth understanding.

Communion with God

"Rejoice evermore. Pray without ceasing," the Apostle Paul wrote by inspiration of God (I Thess. 5:16-17). That these two frames of mind go together was effectively demonstrated by Paul's life.

The record of his life and what he accomplished dramatically illustrates the power of such right thinking.

"Pray without ceasing" indicates a state of mind that is continually attuned to God; that is, He is ever in our thoughts, or in the background of them, and during the day we frequently discuss things with Him. "What should I do here, Lord?" ... "Where did I put that book, Lord?" . . . "Who should I remember in prayer right now, Lord?" ... "Here's a chance to witness, Lord. What should I say?" . . . "I love You, dear Lord. You're the greatest!"

I can testify from personal experience that if the Lord is all-in-all to us, if we "pray without ceasing," then we will rejoice evermore! We can't help but do so, because His presence and continual guidance thrills our hearts with such joy!

Charles H. Spurgeon said, "Communion with God is a great maker of music." Have you taken time out to commune especially with God recently, to listen to Him? What unutterable joy it is to experience a communication you know is from Him! But we have to stop talking sometimes and listen. Then He will give us some of the answers we may be seeking. If His Holy Spirit indwells us, why should we not be able to have this blessed experience?

". . . Remember that true prayer and fellowship with God cannot be all from one side," wrote Andrew Murray. "We need to be still, to wait and hear what response God gives. This is the office of

the Holy Spirit, to be the Voice of God to us."—
The School of Obedience.

The psalmist had the right attitude toward God.
He cried, "My soul longeth, yea, even fainteth for
the courts of the Lord. My heart and my flesh
crieth out for the living God!" (Psa. 84:2).

Later in the same psalm he said, "For the Lord
God is a sun and shield. The Lord will give grace
and glory. No good thing will He withhold from
them that walk uprightly" (Psa. 84:11). The
heart-mind attitude of the former verse assures the
promise of the latter. There's power in right thinking!

Thomas A. Kempis wrote:

> The kingdom of God is peace and joy in the Holy
> Ghost, that is not given to wicked people. Our
> Lord Jesus Christ will come to thee and will
> show thee His consolations. If thou wilt make
> ready for Him in thy heart a dwelling-place, that
> is all He desireth to have in thee, and there is it
> His pleasure to be. Betwixt Almighty God and a
> devout soul there are many ghostly visitings,
> sweet inward speaking, great gifts of grace, many
> consolations, much heavenly peace, and wondrous
> familiarity of the blessed presence of God.—*The
> Imitation of Christ.*

There's power in right thinking!

David Brainerd, one of the greatest missionaries
who ever lived, wrote in 1740, "I enjoyed great
sweetness in communion with my dear Saviour. I
think I never in my life felt such an entire weaned-
ness from this world and so much resigned to God
in everything. Oh, that I may always live to God!"

And many other men who have accomplished great things for God—such as John Wesley, Hudson Taylor, Charles L. Finney, and Dwight L. Moody—have had a similar close walk with God. There's power in right thinking!

Right Thinking

In this book we have considered a number of principles of right thinking that are set forth in God's Word. The ability to put these principles into practice in our lives depends largely upon our yieldness to God, for it is God the Holy Spirit Who gives us the power to overcome immature and wrong ways of thinking.

The Bible says, "Brethren, do not be children (immature) in your thinking; continue to be babes in [matters of] evil, but in your minds be mature [men]" (I Cor. 14:20, Amplified N.T.). Psychiatrists say that many of the emotional and mental problems that men have, stem from immaturity of thinking!

In writing about one of the foremost principles of right thinking—love—the Apostle Paul said, "When I was a child, I spake as a child, I understood as a child, I thought as a child. But when I became a man, I put away childish things" (I Cor. 13:11).

Therefore let us grow in grace and knowledge of the Lord. Let us yield ourselves unreservedly in obedience to Him. Let us put away hostility, pride, fear, wrath, complaining, and all other childish

141

things—let God cleanse our hearts of these foolish remnants of self-centeredness! Let us turn our eyes upon Jesus and seek to be like Him in all things, including single-minded devotion to God.

For God and His Word hold the key to good mental health.